M000308299

PERSONAL BRANDING

IN THE DIGITAL AGE

How to Become a Known Expert,
Thrive and Make a Difference in a
Connected World

FRANCINE BELEYI

nucleus of change
Press

A CIP catalogue record for this book is available from the
British Library

ISBN-978-1-9999259-0-1 (paperback)
ISBN-978-1-9999259-1-8 (eBook)
ISBN-978-1-9999259-2-5 (audiobook)

10 9 8 7 6 5 4 3 2 1
First edition November 2017
Published by nucleus of change Press

For more information visit: www.francinebeleyi.com |
www.personalbrandinginthedigitalage.com

Front cover graphic design by Gwen Zaiter
Book cover design by Francine Beleyi

To my dad, Jacques Pouta Beleyi, who left us this year. He was a man of courage, dedication, with a strong tenacity and a clear vision of the objectives to achieve.

'Que la terre te soit légère.'

PRAISE FOR PERSONAL BRANDING IN THE DIGITAL AGE

"Francine's seven pillars for building a personal brand, especially in the digital age, is a vital must-read. The digital age can make both a positive and negative impact on our personal brands very quickly, and Francine's approach lays out a useful way to manage your brand effectively with high impact case studies for reference."

— *Russ Shaw*, *Founder of Tech London Advocates*

"Francine made the subject of personal branding very appealing, breaking down conventional codes and, hence, making it accessible to everyone. The use of simple yet empowering language to talk about business sets this book apart. The innovative YEANICC™ framework and the author's take on Personal Branding set the bar high and clarify expectations, which are emphatically met throughout the book. The framework can be applied not only to personal branding but to various aspects of life including training, conducting business deals and even in family life. Readers can identify themselves with the varied case studies/spotlights. The book has helped me define Personal branding as Who you are and how to truly make Yourself Visible. My key takeaway is that the BEing trumps the Doing."

— *Komlan Gnamatsi*, *Linguist & Trainer*

"Just occasionally in life, we meet people who can be described as truly remarkable. Francine is just such a person. Throughout her book, her sincere wish to help and empower others to lead happier and more fulfilling lives shines through. An inspiring teacher, her book is an easy to follow step-by-step guide that can help the reader let go of old destructive ways of thinking. It shows ways to use the Internet to reach out to the world combined with the guidance for personal growth. With her kind and sincere guidance, the author paves the way to success for her readers. A truly remarkable book."

— *Stella Duigan*

"Not wanting to be confined by the organisation I have worked in for many years, I took a journey both on a personal and professional level. This book encapsulates the steps of that journey which has worked for me to get me to where I am today. Those wanting to take that same journey of personal transformation will find the YEANICC™ framework of great benefit. The book is able to take the reader of any background, age, professional outlook and personal beliefs on a beautiful journey of self-branding."

— *Vishnu Dass*, COO,
Indra Sistemas Malaysia

"Everyone should read this important book no matter who you are and what you do. Francine Beleyi has introduced some new fundamental concepts as well as relating others in a refreshingly 21st century way. All this is underpinned by the greatest truism about life. The journey of life doesn't make progress without a never-ending investigation in to one's values. As if this isn't enough she adds the dimension of the digital age to such vital and philosophical information. This is a practical and accessible book that one can go back to over and over again."

— *Rod Unger*, *Founder of the charity Dekamile*

CONTENTS

FOREWORD

"Everyone, but particularly the younger generation, face enormous challenges in the world today, and even more in the years ahead. One critical area involves making choices between the vast number of possibilities now associated with personal development. These choices are increasingly linked to the growing impact of the digital world on every aspect of our lives. Francine has produced a thorough and readable tour of the issues. It is one of the first books that attempts to provide insightful advice on both areas and how we can manage these challenges more effectively. The book makes an invaluable contribution to helping us all lead more rewarding lives, beyond the unsustainable obsession with making more and more money. The book should be widely read -- and used, together with the online resources that are associated with it."

—**Dr Bruce Lloyd,** Emeritus Professor of Strategy, London South Bank University

INTRODUCTION

WELCOME TO PERSONAL BRANDING IN THE DIGITAL AGE

Everyone wants to do something meaningful in their life and get paid for it. It doesn't matter if you have an average job, work for a large corporation, or own your company. Making yourself noticed and recognised for your expertise is crucial. However – in order to do it, you will need to make yourself more visible.

That's what this book will do for you – teach you how to utilise your passions and skills in order to have a greater influence and make a difference. There are many ways to do that; we'll get to it in a moment.

First let's address the obvious: 81% of all buyers turn to the Internet to research the products and services they want to purchase. The question is: can you make yourself stand out during this search?

Hundreds of millions of dollars are spent on consumers turning to the Internet to find products and services. From purchasing holidays to seeking health advice, people are looking online for the solution. That's exactly where you come in.

There used to be a time when dedication to a job mattered. Today, you can be on a job for ten, fifteen or twenty years and be let go. In the digital age, it's all about relationship, and it's here where your 'personal brand' comes in. Branding yourself in an effective way can increase your income significantly.

Whether you are an author, small business owner, freelancer, public speaker, consultant, business executive, the list is endless; you need a spotlight shining directly on you. But once it's there, you must have a voice that captures your audience.

- Are you tired of working in an environment where the value you bring to the table is not recognised?
- Do you find yourself often in conflict with people in the organisation you work for?
- Are you frustrated by not getting paid what you deserve?
- Are you struggling to find a way to enjoy what you love and be rewarded for it?
- Are you sick of competing with platforms that 'uberise' your job and commoditise your profession?
- Are you ready to reach the next level in your life by sharing a unique message that will resonate with your audience?

What if there is a way to get out of the rat race that you find yourself in while enabling you to do what you love, with people you love, and getting paid handsomely?

This book will show you the strategies to become a leading voice in your field and attract more opportunities.

It is no longer enough just to have skills to perform your job. You must build up your personal authority if you want to become visible to anyone looking for your expertise.

My goal is to help you become the leading voice in your field so that you enjoy what you do, are rewarded handsomely for it, and make a bigger difference in your world.

I will show you how to develop a distinctive and authentic identity, and how to be confident when standing for what you believe in that makes not only a difference in your life, but in the lives of others.

Personal Branding in the Digital Age is a practical guide where I share my personal experience while going through this process as an individual struggling to find my personal voice, but also as a business owner, a coach, a trainer, a consultant, and a mentor who has helped many individuals and business owners to develop an authentic path to reach their desired destinations.

Through my research, and interviews common patterns emerged, which I encapsulated in the easy and clear framework, YEANICC™ with the 7 pillars anyone can use to lead in their chosen field and get highly paid.

What is Different in this Book?

Most personal branding books give a long list of ideas and things to do without laying out a clear blueprint that is easy and simple to follow. The 7-pillar framework, YEANICC™, encapsulates all my discoveries and knowledge acquired throughout the years of trial-and-error experience. It offers a structured, yet simple guide to building an influential personal brand.

It will help you successfully:
- Understand the building blocks of a personal brand
- Leverage your passion, interests and skills to attract lucrative opportunities
- Avoid wasting time with projects that won't work for you

- Develop, grow and build the value your audience is looking for

You need to take the responsibility to tell people what they need to know about you. That's what developing an authentic personal brand allows you to do.

I believe it's the responsibility of each and every one of us to use our passion, our skills and talents to make a difference in our own lives and to be of service to others, be it in business, in a not for profit organisation, in volunteering and in our daily jobs.

How to Make the Best Use of the Book?

- If you need a complete makeover, go through the steps as presented in the 7-pillar framework, **YEANICC**™. Otherwise, start by taking the Personal Branding assessment, available for free online, to determine which pillars you need to focus on most.
- The accompanying Playbook will help you to craft your own Personal Branding Roadmap, and design a 12-week action plan to quickly start the process.
- The Resources page offers additional materials and planners to achieve your goals faster.
- This practical guide is packed with easy to use concepts, real life examples, case studies, expert tips and action points to complete to get the most out of it quickly. It is for implementers and not a novel.
- If you have a deep desire to implement the YEANICC™ model faster, I invite you to join my private group, the *Leading Voices Circle,* a community where you get access to all the tools, free videos, audio materials, templates and training to launch your own platform to success.

- If you can't wait to discover the incredible teachings I share in this book, head straight to *PersonalBrandingintheDigitalAge.com* where you can watch a video that explains the essential in less than 10 minutes.

The research and writing process has been a great learning curve for me. I don't pretend to have all the answers for your specific situation, but reading this book will take you closer to achieving your goals and more. Join me in this exciting journey.

P.S. If you like what you've read by the close of this book, I would absolutely love to hear from you, get to know you better and have you post a success story, picture or video and comment on the Facebook wall at *fb.me/PersonalBrandingintheDigitalAge*

If you have any questions, email *hello@nucleusofchange.com*

P.P.S. If you enjoy this book and find it useful, I'll be very grateful if you post a short review and your success story on Amazon. Your support makes a difference. I read and respond to all the reviews personally so I can make this book even better. If you'd like to leave a review, just visit this link *PersonalBrandingintheDigitalAge.com*

Thanks again! **Let's start on this journey together.**

PART I: THE FUNDAMENTALS OF PERSONAL BRANDING

'In the digital age, business as usual can no longer be the norm.'

Personal Branding is one of the topics that generate a lot of passion and controversy. Everyone has an opinion of what branding is, or should be, and whether it's useful or deceptive. This is because of the perception and meaning people attach to the word 'branding' and the examples they have personally experienced.

When people hear the word branding, they think about a website, a logo or product. They also think about selfies or photos posted on Facebook or other social media outlets. This is not at all what this book is about.

In this section, I cover what personal branding truly means, what it means for other people and my perspective. I also explain why you should build a personal brand now in the digital age, what stops people from creating a powerful one and how to break through your limitations.

1. What is Branding?

If you look on Twitter, @Virgin business brand has two-hundred-and-thirty-one-thousand followers as of

October 2017. But if you look at the personal account of the owner, @RichardBranson, you'll find that the 'tie-loathing adventurer, philanthropist & troublemaker who believes in turning ideas into reality' as he's described in his profile, has 11.2 million followers. His personal profile attracts fifty times more followers than the company brand. Why is that?

Simply because people buy from people. Richard Branson the man inspires more trust than the business brand. He leverages his personal following to communicate his business message, which is received more favourably by his audience.

- What if you too could speak directly to millions of fans that are eager and waiting to hear from you?
- What if these fans became the ambassadors of your business because they love your ideas and vision?
- What if you had ideal clients willing to spread your message to their friends and network?

Personal branding allows you to do just that.

What Personal Branding is Not?

Personal branding:
- Is not mere self-promotion
- Is not bragging
- Is not being someone you are not
- Is not being vain
- Is not posting selfies on social media

"Personal branding is the practice of people marketing themselves and their careers as brands."
—Wikipedia

Etymologically, to brand was a way of marking property. Why shouldn't you apply the same technique that can help others recognise who you are without confusion or ambiguity?

This is what personal branding means for some professionals and entrepreneurs.

"Personal Branding, to me, is summarised as a defining set of values by which you conduct yourself, and being consistent with those values in everything you do, and in every way you express yourself, whether in written form, in a digital space, with a large audience, or in one-on-one interactions."

—Daniel Gurrola, Telcom senior executive

"It's just being consistent with who you are and what your values are, and by making sure that your actions, your behaviours, and your words are consistent with the values you have. We all have strengths and weaknesses and must understand what they are and be ourselves."

—Russ Shaw, founder of
Tech London Advocates

"For me, on a daily basis, my personal brand represents what I stand for. It's my image, my purpose. It's how I speak. It's my behaviour in public. It's how I talk to someone or how I help an elderly woman cross the road. It's how I conduct myself."

—Naomi Sesay, media specialist
& global speaker

"Personal branding means being your authentic self. People try to brand themselves a bit too much I think, especially with social media. It's about being

proud of your professional accomplishments and sharing the work you do and how you feel about your industry. But I think it's also about being real. Don't pretend to be something you're not. People can smell that."

—Jessica Gioglio, author, speaker, marketing & public relations executive

The common keywords used by these professionals are: be who you are, be true to your values, and be your authentic self. For me, **"Personal branding is not something you do; it's who you are."**

It's about living your values openly and showing the world who you truly are. It enables you to stand out from the crowd, to be easily recognisable, and engage powerfully with your audience.

If you are prepared to be yourself and walk your talk, then personal branding will be a great enabler for your professional success.

- If I say Beyoncé, what comes to your mind? Glamorous singer?
- If I say Obama, what do you say? Charismatic ex-president of the US?
- If I say Richard Branson, you say? Creative, adventurous businessman who has fun in what he does?

These three celebrities are distinct in their personal style, their individual missions, and who they are. You form a clear image in your mind and can use specific words to describe each of them separately just from hearing their names. It should be this same way for you. When someone says your name, a clear image should form in the listener's mind, along with choice words that describe you. The first step is recognising your distinctions and presenting them to the world. It's about sharing compelling stories to make a bigger impact in the most authentic way.

"It's the 'branding' that allows me to touch lives around the world." —Tony Robbins

Personal branding is not only about who you are, but also how other people perceive you. Therefore, it's important that who you are matches how people view you. To check that alignment you need to ask feedback from trusted friends and review testimonials from clients to perform an honest reality check.

Personal Branding is About Being Visible.

People who have made a great impact were able to reach a broader audience because they were visible. Mother Theresa, Nelson Mandela, and Oprah Winfrey leveraged the media to magnify their power.

Sure, there are many people who do great things behind the scenes who aren't visible and, therefore, have a limited reach they could otherwise have if more people knew about them.

EXPERT TIP: Various Ways to Use a Personal Brand | Olivier Zara

Olivier Zara is a management and social media consultant and expert in Collective Intelligence. For him personal branding can be used in two different ways:

1. For money, glory, status and power
2. To achieve a dream and make the world a better place

People are drawn to one or the other end of this spectrum based on their motivations. But he says that following one path doesn't necessarily mean the other aspect will not happen. You can chase your dream and end up accumulating a lot of money and recognition, like Oprah Winfrey, Steve Jobs or Elon Musk. Or you may choose to focus on power and earn a lot of money that you can then use to make the world a better place, like Bill Gates or Warren Buffet.

To build a personal brand, he thinks we should 'share our beliefs and stand for what we believe in.'

Olivier believes in the collective intelligence, with deeply held values of humility. His goal is to work toward the progress of humanity the same way a missionary would. This is reflected in the pedagogic style of his books and blogs. He is the author of 7 books, including "Succeed your Career with Personal Branding," translated from the French title.

From military background to consultant

Olivier hasn't always been a guru of personal branding and collective intelligence. He has his own story of personal transformation. After he graduated from the top French military school EMSAM, he joined the Forces as a finance director and auditor and was sent to Sarajevo during the heat of the conflict.

'When I was coming out of a plane, the bodies of dead soldiers were entering.' he says.

The environment took a toll on him, and when he turned thirty years old, he decided to get back into civilian life. Back to Paris he started job hunting with limited success. He sent hundreds of CVs to various corporations receiving no replies, until he realised that businesses weren't interested in recruiting someone with a military background. Finally, a consultancy firm gave him the break he needed to prove himself.

How Did I Get Interested in Studying Personal Branding?

Back in 2011, it was the 100th anniversary of the International Women's Day. Each year on the 8th of March, all major newspapers and magazines across the world compile individual lists of the most successful women, but I wanted to read something else that year. I wanted to know who were the Black women making a difference in Europe and could inspire me and other people like myself.

There wasn't much information around to look out for at the time, so I decided to create my own list, applying the famous quote from Mahatma Gandhi, 'Be the change you want to see in the world!'

I asked friends, acquaintances and members of the public to nominate women of African origin in Europe who they found inspirational. These women lacked visibility, and although their achievements are recognised by their peers, their names and faces often remain confidential. I received a positive response. People submitted the names of those they knew who made some difference in their community.

I put together the first list of the 20 Inspirational Women from African Diaspora in Europe (ADIPWE). I also created a *LinkedIn group* which today has more than three-hundred women and men interested in sharing inspirational stories.

People who have nominated these women felt compelled to do so because of what they stand for and what they were doing in their community.

And a brand is exactly that: who you are, what you do, why, and how you do it. It's about what you stand for and what you deliver every single day.

A few months after the publication of that first list, I was invited to speak at the first African Women's conference in London on ... Personal branding!

In case you are still not sure why you should build a personal brand, let me give you a few reasons why you should consider it.

2. Why Should You Build a Personal Brand in a Digital Age?

If your high-powered job suddenly terminated today, will the people you worked with while employed still pick up the phone to talk to you?

Unfortunately, for most people, the answer is no. When you are in an influential, corporate job or work for an influential company, you receive many invitations to attend the fanciest events, prestigious meetings, speaking gigs, etc.

But as soon as you leave your influential job, the invites dry out and you slide back into anonymity. Suddenly, you are nobody. You don't get invitations anymore. Your calls are not returned. You struggle to set up meetings with prospects. This scenario is what often happens unless you were able to strategically build a personal reputation and were recognised as an expert by your name alone and not particularly the name of the company you worked for.

If you are a business owner, you may wonder why you should build a personal brand. After all, what you sell are products and services. But you should, because there is a hidden element you are not taking into consideration. Consider the case of Richard Branson described earlier.

You may say that not everyone is as charismatic as Sir Branson. This is true, but everyone is different and have something unique they can use to connect with their desired audience, which we will see later in this book.

Unless you are an investigative journalist, working on a sensitive subject, or a spy who needs to keep your profile under the radar, almost any professional, entrepreneur, freelancer, and executive should focus on building their personal brand first, and then their business second. Why?

Because you can fail or terminate a business or a career, but your personal brand lasts a lifetime. You significantly increase the odds of launching a successful start-up when you have a reputation and followers behind you.

Contrary to popular belief, you are more likely to raise funds in a crowdfunding campaign if you already have a community to leverage on. I will elaborate on this topic in part 3 when addressing the monetisation strategies.

Close to half of the population is online today and those people are searching for solutions to problems they face. But there is a lot of noise and scams that make it difficult to distinguish who is genuine and who is not.

How do you ensure that you attract the right opportunities in this busy environment?

You must be more visible than the average person and be recognised as an expert in your field.

An influential personal brand helps you to:

• Be visible and attract opportunities to achieve your goals faster

Be found by clients and people who need your services and expertise. You become the go-to-person.

Be trusted by your prospects or anyone you meet or have scheduled to meet, because you have an online presence that they can personally check out. Finding and checking you out online reassures people that you are a genuine person that other people know and trust. In today's world of scammers, not having an online presence is suspicious. People tend to think you may have something to hide!

What do you do when you have a meeting with someone you know nothing about? You Google the person and check for more information.

• Attract the right kind of people to build your tribe

We are moving from the information age into the relationship age, a world where engagement with communities is the golden currency, where emotion and connection are highly prized and valued. We are social animals. People and brands that are able to give emotion and connect with their audience will be the winners in the relationship age.

• Make sales dramatically easier and increases your income

You get paid more whether as a consultant, speaker or executive. You become a credible source of information in your field. Examples in this book will show you how.

• People make friends with people, not with brands

There are other reasons personal branding is the right thing to do. People have their favourite brands, but those are not considered as friends. People will relate more to a human being than a faceless brand, like Sir Branson's case shows.

• Build your reputation

Your brand is your reputation. That is what people say about you when you're not in the room.

Take control of what you want to be out in the public space, so when people search or Google you, they get the information you want them to see.

To be visible you need to be distinct and inspire people to trust you, your ideas, and your philosophy, to buy from you, to buy your ideas and philosophy, and join forces with you. You need to be known, trusted and preferred. I am going to show how to do this and it's easier than you think. It only needs to be thought out strategically, first.

Being different is your biggest strength.

We are all different and that's what makes the world interesting. It is okay to get inspiration from others to broaden your mind on what is possible, but don't try to be like anyone else. If two of you are the same, one is unnecessary.

One person's winning formula might be the losing formula for someone else if they don't have the same personality, resources, skills and passion. And realistically, it's unlikely you will achieve this kind of similarities.

Having your own unique brand makes you more visible and allows you to attract people who resonate with you and your values. It's also a good way to let people select themselves based on your values rather than you having to do this job for them.

Personal branding applies to all professions, all sectors, and all communities, whether you are an investor, a journalist, a diplomat or an artist.

Tim Dawson, president of the National Union of Journalists (NUJ) and author of Make eBooks Pay says:

"Your reputation and what people know of you is what generates interest in your work and I think it's something people should think about: how to interact on social media, how they present in public. It's very important.

"We work in a very challenging industry where people find their employment chance evaporating, at short notice sometimes, having a strong personal branding; having a way of communicating directly to an audience is an insurance against that. It means that if you stop working for broadcaster A, or a newspaper Y and you want to take some of your audience with you, you have the means of doing so. It's a bit of luxury not to think about that."

- **Make a bigger impact, a bigger difference in the world**

"If you don't share your gift, the world gets sick."
—Carol Fitzgerald

An influential personal brand draws people to you because it touches their lives. When they connect with you, it's the same as becoming a family member or close friend.

3. What Stops People from Creating a Personal Brand?

• Deeply engrained beliefs from culture

Branding is considered as superficial in certain cultures and environments. They believe if they work hard enough their work will speak for itself and they will be recognised. Nothing can be farther from the truth.

Today, anyone can be known through their content and become an influencer. You no longer need to wait to be accepted by a book publisher to publish a book or wait to be invited by a TV programme because you can share your content on YouTube. You no longer need to be published by a newspaper; you can publish your own blog, contribute on other influencers' blogs or write on platforms such as Medium, LinkedIn, etc. You no longer need to go to a radio station; you can publish your audio content on iTunes, SoundCloud and other podcasts platforms.

We will cover this in more detail in Pillar #6. What you need to create is **trust** with the people you are looking to influence by being a reliable source of information, and by nurturing the relationships you create with your audience, and by remaining transparent and open.

• I don't want to share my private life

I am often asked if someone can be an influencer without sharing their personal life.

You don't need to share your private life online to be a respected influencer, but you do need to share what you believe in, your purpose, your vision, and values and not necessarily what you do in your private life.

Building an authentic personal brand doesn't mean you should talk about everything in your life. You must be strategic, because people will use the information you publish to judge you. It's about being intentional in how you choose to present yourself.

As a rule of thumb, you should assume that anything you share online will find its way in the public domain; therefore, sharing a mix of professional and personal information that you are happy for someone to know about you is okay, but do remember to protect your privacy.

Some people make the choice to share their personal life without restrictions. It's their choice and about what they're trying to achieve.

You can intelligently share a mix of your personal and professional life to achieve your objectives without telling every single detail about your life.

"You don't have to be stiff. You can be human and have a life and showcase that you're having fun, because if you're too stiff and boring who's going to pay attention to you? I think it's a mix of being professional, but also infusing personality and showing that you're human as well. So that's really what I abide by in everything from my appearance to the things I do online. I don't get too hung up on it." —Jessica Gioglio

People like Richard Branson, Tony Robins, Oprah Winfrey, Marie Forleo or Brendon Burchard have all built great personal brands by sharing their purpose, but you don't know much about their private lives, do you?

• Personal branding is just marketing

I know someone who hates all forms of marketing. He even dismisses authors who promote their book that teach valuable insights from years of research. How on earth is that author supposed to pass on their knowledge if they don't publish a book and promote it to the people who need it?

Marketing is a tool for influence. It can be used for good or bad. Unfortunately, it has been used for less noble purposes, so people have become wary. But like a knife, which can be used for either purposes of cutting meat or stabbing someone, marketing is being used to either benefit or deceive. I hope you will use this knowledge to benefit people.

• You build your brand when you are selling something

Start building your brand today. You can start right where you are and before you create a product to sell, and whether you are a stay-at-home mum with a passion of starting a business, or if you're a high-flying banker dreaming of starting a gourmet bakery, or a small business owner dreaming of someday building an empire.

• I am too old to start building my brand

There is no age limit to start building your brand. One influential CEO, who is more than seventy years old, hired a consultancy firm to write his memoir and to create an online presence for him as a legacy for his children and grandchildren.

A lot of people have made it after forty, and even later in life. What are your excuses?

Vera Wang, who is today one of the world's premier women's designers, was a figure skater and journalist before entering the fashion industry at age forty.

Julia Child worked in advertising and media before writing her first cookbook when she was fifty, launching her career as a celebrity chef in 1961.

Charles Darwin spent most of his life as a naturalist who kept to himself, but in 1859 at age fifty, his book, "On the Origin of Species," changed the scientific community forever.

• I don't have anything unique

Your experiences are your greatest lessons. What you've learned along the way gives you the authority to be the expert of your life. Everyone is on a different path. What you take for granted is something someone is struggling with.

I have a friend who is intellectually smart but doesn't know how to cook. If you know how to cook well, and for you it's a no brainer, you may be able to teach her your ten best recipes step-by-step to help her and other people like her. Now you're the expert about something you previously took for granted. She will be able to host a party for friends or for a loved one simply by using your menu courses.

In fact, Amélie et Sébastien Guinamant, co-founder of *Cook'n Box*, took this concept further, selling you all the menu pieces pre-cut. You only need to put them in an oven and host the most sophisticated dinner at home without paying more than if you've done the shopping yourself.

There are tons of examples like these where people struggled to come up with something unique about themselves, because they have lived too long viewing themselves the same way. It shouldn't be that way, and we will later see at least six different methods you can use to find your uniqueness.

• I sell products, so I don't need to be an expert

Do you have to decide to become an expert rather than focus on creating products that are scalable? I don't think they are mutually exclusive. They can be complementary. You can use your personal brand to educate your audience far better than a faceless organisation can.

• If I start, I must live up to high expectations

Some people are afraid to be held accountable. I met an inspiring speaker and followed up with him some time afterward to see what he was doing to take what he shared with us.

I was surprised when he revealed he didn't have time to carry on his vision. After further investigation, I discovered the real reason was he didn't want to be held accountable to his vision in case it took too long to happen.

Just because you have a vision doesn't mean you are a prisoner of it or you have to be perfect. Someone who frequently has big visions is Elon Musk, the boss of Tesla. But he also gives them away, so others can carry them forward as he did with the Hyperloop.

People who believe in your vision are more likely to join forces with you to carry it forward. Avoid the naysayers and don't put too much pressure on yourself.

4. Why People Fail to Act Even When they Know they Should?

Take an honest assessment of yourself. What is holding you back to do what you really want to achieve? Do you sometimes say to yourself, "who do you think you are?" Do you find yourself procrastinating, researching and learning everything you can without putting any of them in application?

It all starts with our mindset. Success is 80% psychology and 20% effort. Having the right mindset is crucial to our success.

You may have an issue with promoting yourself because of an aversion of being self-centred. When you shift your focus and know what you are doing is about serving others, you can no longer hold back.

It's a question of having the right perspective and a big enough why as we will see in Pillar #1. Look at your deep motivation and why you want to take this journey of personal branding in the first place.

• Limiting Beliefs

You need to get rid of the limiting beliefs that have prevented you from achieving your desired goals so far. Ask yourself, **how strongly do you believe in yourself** and in what you want to put out there?

• Lack of Confidence

You need to build the confidence to grow your personal brand and share it with the world. For that you have to be willing to be open to people, show them who you really are, and believe in what you are doing.

So how can you develop that confidence? One tool I used with great success for myself and my clients is the **competence-confidence loop**.

The things we often do are at the forefront of our consciousness whilst other things we are not aware of sit in the background of our consciousness.

Suppose you are driving a car you've had for many years on the motorway. You've done this journey many times. You feel safe and confident driving and don't have to think about it. You are doing it automatically. You are unconsciously competent.

However as soon as you get in a new situation or drive a new car, let say a Tesla, you may realise what you took for granted with your old car. You cannot do the same thing as before. You become conscious of your incompetence.

Through trial and error and some practice, you consciously become competent again. But this has required your full attention and the tasks performed have been at the forefront of your consciousness.

After a while, you become unconsciously competent again and drive your Tesla without thinking about it anymore. You are totally confident in your ability and you start dreaming again on the motorway whilst driving. The competence-confidence loop is closed.

This is a simple yet powerful technique to use to develop confidence in your ability to get what you need to be done.

Some years ago, one of my clients was starting her business and hired me to be her mentor and coach to grow her business. She was a hard-working lady, but used to doubt her ability to succeed, especially when she had to do something she's never done before.

I helped her break her self-doubts. She had never started a business nor created a marketing strategy. I showed her how to create one and plan the activities that will help her to keep on track. When she did it once, she was confident to run with it. Then she had to organise an exhibition that she has never done before. We worked together to pull it off and it was a great success.

What she seemed to suffer from wasn't competence, but the confidence to do what she had never done before. Once she did it, she felt confident to do it next time.

This is the same for you. You can leverage on your past ability to succeed to anchor that knowledge and confidence and achieve any goal you want.

Self-doubt can be paralysing and over accentuated when you are by yourself. Having an accountability partner who can push you to do things you won't otherwise do is important.

If you don't have anyone around you, able to take a helicopter view to make you see the beautiful land in front of you, you may miss your destiny!

• Comparison

Don't look at successful people and assume they have been an overnight success. The truth is there is no such a thing as an overnight success. They would have been working hard for many years before getting their breakthrough. They have their own challenges, struggles and self-doubt.

Be inspired by successful people, but take your own journey. It is vitally important to develop and maintain confidence in what you do and who you are. Internalising a philosophy of self-acceptance helps you avoid putting yourself down when something is not perfectly done and be able to move forward.

You are neither superior nor inferior to someone else who is having or not having success. You are just a fallible, imperfect human being who refuses to rate yourself based on your actions and past successes but only focusses on those aspects of yourself you wish to change.

Without self-acceptance, you will continue to denigrate yourself and fail to solve the problem. If you cannot overcome your problem by yourself, you may seek professional help. Take each step one by one until you are ready to fly. Don't get impatient.

• Fear

I've realised that behind strong, ambitious and driven people also lies fear, self-doubt, and criticism of not being good enough. The most critical people are those who have achieved a lot already in life, but have this insatiable need to move forward and do more.

I had an honest and sincere conversation with someone I admire and respect. And I am gobsmacked to realise that this is not the confident person I thought he was. This person has helped a lot of entrepreneurs grow and build 7-8 figure income and thriving businesses. But himself? He is barely doing what he really wants to do in life. He admits that his dream is to become a full-time professional speaker, but he doesn't have a website or a speaker reel to show prospective event organisers his capabilities.

Okay. I know some people don't have those assets and still thrive on word of mouth recommendations. But in a digital age, having a website to showcase your authority should be a no brainer. So, what's holding him back, I wonder? Why hasn't he already put up a website that was due to be completed two years ago? I could easily help him to *create an online presence* in less than a month, as I've done for many other people. And I did offer him that, but even then, he didn't take up my offer. Why?

The reality is between what we know and what we do there's sometimes a gap, and beneath our lack of action there is often fear. It can be any kind of fear: fear of not being good enough, fear of being judged, fear of loss, fear of the process, fear that others know best, fear of failure, and I can go on and on.

Fear of success

It might feel strange that I am talking about fear of success. But in fact, many studies show it's not only fear of not being good enough that prevent people from moving forward, but also fear of success.

Fear of failure

'What if I start this and I fail?' Well, as the lottery says, you have to be in it to win it. Not taking the journey is the surest way not to get there. You have to be willing to take the risk, a calculated one. Think about your 'opportunity cost.' What are you losing if you don't change? How much more could you be earning with a stronger and authentic personal brand? What do you miss by settling for less financially, emotionally, intellectually and spiritually?

Fear of asking

Don't be afraid to ask for what you want and deserve. Get out of the 'not-for-profit' mindset where you give, give and give. I have nothing against the not for profit sector.

One of my values is to give back; what I am saying is to have a balance. You must sustain yourself for the long haul. So be more strategic.

It's best to help a few people than trying to help everyone and failing miserably and losing your steam. Ask for what you want, increase your price or negotiate your first salary increase.

The most important thing we can do is be true to ourselves and do whatever it takes to identify our fears and take action to mitigate it. Many famous artists and well-known people admit to still being afraid to go on stage, but they have developed a technique to do it anyway. The book "Feel the Fear and Do It Anyway" by Susan Jeffers is a good resource.

My recommendation is: do it afraid. Don't wait to be more confident, it may be too late. The bottom line is that if we do not identify and sort out what is holding us back, we will miss the boat.

• Lack of discipline – procrastination

Discipline and good habits are key elements for success. We need to do what we must do consistently to get the results we desire, whether we feel like it or not.

What great habits will help us move the needle one bit at a time and achieve our overall goals?

The problem is we are creatures of habits and it can be very difficult to change deeply rooted habits we've used to. But we have to ask ourselves what will be the consequences of not changing to get us on the way.

In the final part of this book on mindset, you will find useful strategies to reclaim your power and tools for productivity.

PART II: THE 7 PILLARS TO CREATE AN INFLUENTIAL PERSONAL BRAND

How do You Sell When You Are the Product?

This question elicits emotional issues, fears, and resistance for those who are not comfortable with this prospect. I started looking for answers since 2008 after I quit my job to start my own consultancy, *nucleus of change.* To sell anything you need to know the product inside and out and be able to talk about it. If you don't know what makes you tick, or what your motivation is, or what makes you unique, you are doomed to failure.

When I started my job in marketing, the first thing the company did was to take me through a product training. They explained the products and services they offered, who they sold to, what clients loved about them, and what made the company different from their competitors. It was important to understand these elements of the product to create effective marketing strategies that spoke clearly to each of the different segments of clients.

The same goes for you. If you want to market yourself effectively and get people's attention, you ought to start by understanding the product—you—inside and out, and the value you provide to others.

I remember arguing about a feature that was supposed to provide a great benefit to the user. I didn't think it was providing much value, but I've since learned the mistake I was making. It wasn't about me, but what the customer valued and is prepared to pay to get it.

Many people make the same mistake. They project their expectations onto the customer, ignoring what that person really values.

You got to be sold on the product you are selling to be able to sell it confidently.

Personal branding is about clearly defining who you are by communicating your value effectively to the audience you care about. Your audience can be a company that you're pitching to, or customers, or potential partners.

I am proposing a powerful journey of self-discovery, where you will rediscover who you are and what makes you feel alive. You need to sort this out to be able to progress smoothly in your life. You can get away with living your life accidentally for a while, but sooner or later this yearning will come back to bite you and force you to take the necessary time to find out about what you love.

After ten years of personal research and interviewing successful people, I've discovered several key methods for living your purpose and how to overcome the stumbling blocks that appear along the way. I am going to share with you my discoveries and how to navigate your way and take control of your life by developing an authoritative personal brand.

Unless you stop to examine your life and understand yourself deeply, you are unlikely to project a strong and authentic brand. **Personal branding starts with credibility.**

That is why you must define and communicate clearly who you are, what is important to you, why you do what you do, your story, and what makes you stand out from everyone else.

To be a thoughtful leader, you must have a point of view, express yourself with perspective and speak effectively about your convictions.

Personal branding is anything, except a linear process. But it shouldn't be complicated to create an authentic personal brand. Many people are confused without a clear step-by-step methodology to follow.

The ground breaking 7-pillar framework, YEANICC™, is an easy and a step-by-step process to guide you through the key aspects to clarify in order to build an influential personal brand that will boost your professional goals.

The 7 YEANICC™ Pillars are:
- Pillar #1 Know **Y**ourself
- Pillar #2 Master Your **E**xpertise
- Pillar #3 Know Your **A**udience
- Pillar #4 Lead Your **N**iche
- Pillar #5 Control Your **I**mage
- Pillar #6 **C**onnect with Empathy
- Pillar #7 Build Your **C**ommunity

THE 7 PILLARS OF PERSONAL BRANDING IN THE DIGITAL AGE

YEANICC™

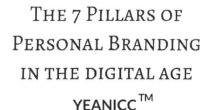

It's not a rigid framework and my intention is not to use it in a dogmatic way. You can complete the steps in any order you wish. But if you are looking for a complete makeover or to re-evaluate where you are in your life, I advise to follow the 7 pillars in the order they are presented, as each pillar builds on the next. If you are already clear about the aspects you want to work on, you can pick and choose the pillars you feel you need to work on.

You can also take the free Personal Branding Assessment, YEANICC™ Index, to determine your score in each pillar and see where to focus in priority.

At the end of this section, you should be able to create your own Personal Branding Execution Roadmap_aligned with your values and build awareness around it.

Pillar #1 Know Yourself

"Your job is to find your calling⋯" —Oprah Winfrey

Unless you stop to examine your life and understand yourself on a deeper level, you are unlikely to project a strong and authentic brand.

Personal branding starts with credibility. That is why you must define and communicate clearly who you are, what you want, what is important to you, why you do what you do, and what makes you stand out from the crowd.

To inspire others, you must know yourself. To be a true leader you must have a point of view, can express yourself with originality, and can speak effectively and frequently about your convictions.

This first pillar, Know Yourself, is the necessary foundation without which it's impossible to build a lasting personal brand. It allows you to be who you truly are, no more and no less, and work from a place of empathy.

I believe that we all have a purpose in life that we yearn to achieve.

We all care about something. Whether we are conscious of it or not, whether we choose to embrace it or discount it, sooner or later, it comes knocking at our door. At first, it knocks quietly, but over time it becomes louder and louder and we no longer can ignore it. We know that it's time to act and be what we are called to be. I call it '**rising to our greatness.**'

Life doesn't always go according to plan, and you can find yourself in a position where you need to re-evaluate your life, open a new chapter and let go of the past.

Sometimes, it's a conscious choice in taking this step—when you figure out what you are doing is not working as you wish. Other times, it's imposed on you by the death of a loved one, a redundancy or another circumstance.

"I remember vividly when my manager called me into the office. I found myself with the HR person who told me my services were no longer needed."

Daniel Gurrola, a senior Telco executive, found himself suddenly unemployed after the company he worked for went through a reorganisation. A graduate from HEC, a top French business school, Daniel enjoyed an uninterrupted career as a top Telco Executive, working in major corporations, top consultancies and was VP of Strategic Engagement before it all suddenly ended.

"Typically, you think you're prepared for this, but you're not, and you find yourself in a situation you have never been in before. There's a bit of a stigma in society when someone is in transition or unemployed. You ask yourself what should I be doing? Should I tell people? What should I tell my family and what should I do? Where do I even start? All these questions come to your mind and you're confused about where to go. How would people perceive you now and what your social circle will become?"

Daniel decided to take advantage of this transition to go on a journey of self-discovery to rediscover himself and dig down into his values and aspirations before jumping into the next venture.

The cost of not knowing yourself is simply not living to your full potential.

It is incredibly sad to encounter fatalist individuals, people who try to discourage others who want more in life. I met a woman who was presenting an economic report. During the Q&A session, she said: 'Loads of people settle for what is available and what is possible rather than what they aspire to do. That is life. I think people have to become pragmatic sometimes, especially when they get married and have children.'

When I heard that, I froze. What a pessimistic and self-limiting view. I think, on the contrary, we need to shoot for the moon regardless of how old we are and whatever responsibilities we have. We cannot resign to live an inferior life and must strive to do amazing things while we're still breathing.

Of course, there is a difference between 'wish' and 'hope.' One is without any ground while the other is based on realistic plans to make our desires happen.

Take Sean Stephenson. He was born with a rare bone disorder. Doctors told his parents he only had twenty-four hours to live. Now Sean is three-feet tall, has fragile bones, and uses a wheelchair, but despite many adversities, he is a motivational speaker and a recognised therapist. He has reached millions of people around the world and spends time with some of the top celebrities. In this TEDx talk, *the prison of your mind*,[1] the thirty-eight-year-old advises, 'Never believe a prediction that doesn't empower you.'

If Sean can adapt to such adverse circumstances, what are your excuses not to?

Other uncompromising people include Elon Musk, Steve Jobs, Bill Gates and Jeff Bezos. They are people who never gave up their dreams to settle for only what other people thought was possible.

Elon Musk dreamt of putting people on Mars and until then made Tesla electric vehicles a reality, bringing together technology, power and environmental friendliness.

Steve Jobs wanted to design the most beautiful tech gadgets, and now we have the iPhone, iTunes and iMac ecosystem of products.

Bill Gates dreamt of seeing at least one computer in every home in America. Today, the average household in the US has five connected devices. [2]

Jeff Bezos believed in Amazon's potential to make money way past the due time. Today, he is one of the richest men on the planet. [3]

If these people didn't believe in their dreams, believe they could achieve the impossible and work relentlessly to make it happen, the world would certainly look very differently today.

I won't deny that sometimes we just need a job to pay the bills, but this doesn't mean we must settle for things we don't feel passionate about. And you should certainly not give up because you are married or have children. In fact, a lot of people start their businesses as a parent, especially women who are called 'mumpreneurs.'

A report from the economic think tank, Development Economics, has evaluated the contribution of 'mumpreneurs' to the UK. It found that "the sector is growing at an unprecedented rate," generating £7bn for the UK economy.[4] By 2025, the report claims that the mum economy will generate £9.5bn for the UK.

Find Your Gift and Shoot for the Moon

Most people often sleepwalk through life, unaware of the gifts they possess and unable to identify them. As a result, they only do what other people want them to do rather than purposefully use their talent to live a more fulfilled life and help others.

We are entering a new era where more and more people are seeking more meaningful careers, and are looking inward to identify their gifts and develop them to be the best in their chosen field, make more money, and have a larger impact on everyone they come in contact with. The worst thing a person can do is settle into an unfulfilling lifestyle without trying to find their hidden treasures and not finding out the difference they can make in their lives and the lives of others.

Not everyone is an entrepreneur and not everyone can study STEM subjects, which most initiatives are currently pushing young people towards. You must find out what your strengths are and choose the best environment so you can thrive in today's world.

I believe that each of us has the power and the ability to trace our individual destinies, but to get there you must know yourself. By knowing who you are, you have the confidence to use your strengths to make the world a better place. To discover your true self, you must follow your intuition and do what you love and not what other people think you should do. How can you bring love into the world if you are unhappy in what you do?

> ### SPOTLIGHT: Naomi Sesay | Knowing Yourself Comes from Within

Naomi Sesay has a multifaceted background. She started her career working for MTV News Networks before she left the company to become a freelance producer/director for production houses, and became one of the first producers for Endemol's *Big Brother*. She also became a property investor, a professional public speaker and ran many projects such as 'What the Bleep Do We Know,' 'The Law of Intention,' and 'The Billionaire Ladies Club.'

Naomi currently works at *Media Trust* where she heads Youth Media Engagement and a team of media trainers who train young people to create, shoot and edit powerful content using their Smartphone.

How did she bring together all her previous activities into her new role?

"I was hugely passionate about all those areas and I felt I could lend myself to them in a very special way. That's why I went for them, especially getting into TV. When I was younger I wanted to be an actress, but my mother said no. So, the next best thing for me was becoming a presenter or producer /director, and that's why I pursued it.

"Becoming a property investor was because I wanted financial freedom. I didn't find that in television and I realised that you can never become wealthy working for somebody else. What I always joke about is you're just over broke, which is a job. It's something that you can only do if you are content with living with a monthly wage. I wasn't. I wanted to have a vast empire and that's what I desired to create with property.

"But what happened was I have gone back to my beginnings. When I was a young child, I understood that we're more than just wealth, we are more than just the things we do.

"We absolutely have something inside us that is trying to get out and that's what I was trying to get out by following these paths. This is where I looked into quantum physics and where I got into spirituality, if you will, but in a way that was proven by science, and accepted, and had been practiced for years by Eastern mythology.

"Those passions came together in a very natural way and it's what I do right now.

"In terms of knowing themselves, people try to 'do' things to know themselves. My ethos is to try and 'be' something to know yourself. And how I do that is by understanding why I am on Earth in the first place and what my purpose is! Once you understand what your purpose is you can do anything you want. You can become the president, you can do road sweeping, you can become the executive of a company, and you can become a graphic designer, knowing that whatever you do, your purpose is being fulfilled."

"Knowing yourself has to come from within. It cannot come from the things that you do, only the things that you become."

How do you go about BEing something?

"My purpose is to raise the level of consciousness to create global peace. I know it sounds very big, but everything I do is to inspire, to motivate or to be a catalyst to someone who thinks, "Oh my, God! I've got it.'

"They open their eyes and feel emotional when they realise 'this is what I'm here to do.' I'm not here to work for somebody, per say. I'm not here to create that, per say. I'm here to do something that gives a wider aspect of who I am.

"I'm here to give love. I'm here to give happiness. I'm here to give solace. I'm here to give comfort, so that fulfils something very integral in the human psyche. And that purpose always carries that aspect.

"If you look at Mother Theresa, she was a very poor woman, but her purpose was to go out and help people and she remained in that state of mind because it fulfilled who she truly was.

"I do many types of exercises for people to help them reach that inner self, but mainly it's sitting down and saying to yourself, 'What do I do best and why?' and that 'why' is quite important.

"So, you could say I love hairdressing, I love playing with different types of designs in people's hair. But why? People will say, 'Because I'm good at it.' No, but why? Keep on drilling; drill down, because at the end you'll get to something even bigger. You'll get to something that says, 'Because I love to make people happy.'

"Purpose is always about somebody else. It's not about you. "

What or Who Is It You Care About?

Do you care about a group of people or a cause? What are you doing to contribute or to advance the cause you care about? How many times have you dismissed your calling and played small? How many times did you go for the easiest solution? And how much longer are you going to stay in that dead-end job or business instead of flying and achieving your highest purpose?

I know it's not always crystal clear. Some people find this process easier than others. This is why I want to shine a bit of light on this journey of self-discovery.

The challenge for you is to believe you are enough and have enough value to share with people who care about the same things you do, and acknowledge that you too are worthy of having a bigger, better life, and can help others achieve the same.

However, I must warn you. There is no recipe for success in this book. Everybody is different and we all follow different paths in life. Some people find their calling at five years old, while others struggle to find what they want to do until later in life.

I've struggled to find my authentic path in life, but after decades of exploration, search and discovery, I found some of the secrets successful people have used for many years to build their empire and live an abundant life.

STORY: A Long Journey of Self-Discovery

I love learning and always seek new challenges to take on. I've explored profession after profession. I've had eleven jobs in the first fifteen years of my professional life. When I set my eyes on a new career, I will do whatever it takes to get into it. I would learn everything I could about my new career and put all my energy into getting the desired job, only to find out a couple of years later it wasn't something I wanted to do for the rest of my life.

I get bored and looked for my next challenge. I was unable to stick to one job and failed to capitalise on any skill as I moved sideways to a totally different field and learned another skill.

As time went on, I expected to find something interesting enough to stick to, but this pattern didn't stop. Instead it intensified. The longest I stayed in a job was four years before I felt the urge to get out and do something different. If you've been there, you know what I'm talking about. If you haven't, you might be thinking what an unstable person!

I became more and more dissatisfied, because I really was trying to find my 'thing.' I knew that although I was okay with what I did, I was far from using my full potential and wanted to do something about it.

The problem was I had no clue what could keep me focussed for more than four years. I didn't know my real passion other than the fact that I enjoyed exploring and challenging myself with new jobs. But these were jobs that didn't necessarily fit my natural talent or abilities. In fact, some of them were the complete opposite of what I would have done naturally.

I became really frustrated that I was not truly using my natural abilities to make a difference in my own life and in the world. I had asked an old boss for feedback during one of my 360-degree assessments. He told me I was immature to keep searching for my path even though I was in my 30s. He felt I should have known by then what I wanted to do.

But the problem was I still didn't know what my natural talent was, because I've spent my whole life exploring multiple careers and learning a range of seemingly unrelated stuff. I was stuck.

I was busy exploring so many options; I got totally lost and forgot what I loved. Has this ever happened to you? It took me many years to rediscover myself, thousands of hours of personal development, seminars, reading books and listening to audiobooks. I took countless personality profiling tests and assessments to uncover my natural flow and rediscover my path. It was a long and painful journey of self-discovery.

I spent my time playing so many games that weren't mine. You see, when you play someone else's game you can never win. Others will always be better at it and beat you with less effort. The best thing to do is to find your own path, create your own game and win every time you play. That is what this book is all about. To help you uncover your true self and not pretending to be someone you're not.

Before I continue, I must let you know something important that many people will not tell you. There is a cost attached to following a path of self-discovery.

You have to commit fully to follow this path, no matter what. Nothing happens in life without a cost. But what is the cost if you continue doing what you don't like and end up frustrated, depressed, and unhappy, rather than paying the price to follow your passion and something that makes you content?

The pain of staying in my job was greater than the cost of leaving, so in 2008, I decided to leave my corporate job, reclaim my freedom and find my path. I embarked on a journey of self- discovery, to follow my flow and do what I love rather than living accidentally.

I started my independent consultancy, nucleus of change, to help people manage and adapt to changes in their business and personal lives, then realised I had the gift to inspire people to clarify their goals, to take immediate action on what they have been putting off for years, and help them to change the course of their lives.

But starting this new venture wasn't smooth sailing. I had to figure many things out along the way. I had to learn how to find my niche, which was a huge struggle for someone who wanted to help everyone. Mistake number one in business: you cannot help everyone. I learned that the hard way. I also struggled to communicate a specific and compelling message that justified why people should do business with me.

Those who did business with me nevertheless were satisfied, but I had no system to keep getting new clients or be referred by previous clients. After months of struggle, I actively started looking for answers to what wasn't working and observed what other successful business owners were doing differently from me. I was willing to pay the price to learn what I didn't know.

SPOTLIGHT: Ekene Som Mekwunye | Award-Winning Filmmaker

"My joy as a filmmaker is being able to put into pictures African stories that could only be told in words."

When Ekene realised the power of films and how effective they can be used to influence people, he decided to affect society with his films.

He says he gets paid to have fun. But it hasn't always been that way. Before he went into film-making, he graduated in business management from the University of Lagos. He worked in island side of Lagos and lived on the mainland, commuting across the longest bridge in Africa like millions of others, stacked in buses in some of the most congested traffic in the world.

One day, he had enough and was no longer willing to endure that rat race. He decided to go after his passion, following a favourite quote from Confucius, 'Find a job you love and you never work again in your life.'

"Life is too short to live another person's life and not do what you enjoy. With every profession in the world, somebody has made a lot of money from it, whether it's painting, rice cooking, anything...The only question is how well can you do that thing?"

"If you are skilled in painting but don't know how to make money from it, know that there are pieces of artwork that have sold for millions of dollars. If you like to clean but don't know how much you can make from it, there are businesses that offer cleaning services to some of the top companies in the world, and they get paid a lot of money.

"I hear people talk about their fear of launching out, but the truth is there is no business that makes money the day it starts. There is a growth stage where things get rough, and that waiting period can be one year, it can be five years, or ten, but you have to grow during that period if you want to make a success of it. And that period is usually a very difficult time. There is no growth stage that is easy. That is what most people don't want to go through and why they remain stuck where they are in their daily 9-to-5.

"If you want to do something, you must be prepared. Like Jesus said in the Bible: 'No man decides to build his house without counting the cost first.' It's going to cost you, but **that's the price you have to pay for your happiness.** And at the end of the day, you realise that it's worth it. I took that journey and today I am very glad I did."

What Is Important to You and How Do You Act Upon It?

It is important to do what you love and align your objectives. Your happiness shouldn't depend on external circumstances. You need to find it from within.

Define what success looks like to you by applying the Habit 2 'Begin with the end in mind' of Stephen Covey's *The 7 habits of highly effective people.*

But you also need to consider the perception of others. After all, you are not living on a desert island. If you aren't in a room and people are talking about you, what would they say? Which words would they use to describe you? Are those the same words you use to describe yourself?

A personal brand is what people say when you are not in the room. So, define how you want people to talk about you. This is what this first pillar, 'Know Yourself,' is all about. To better understand yourself and reflect on your ideal lifestyle. The self-reflecting activities, visualisation and brainstorming exercises proposed below will enable you to think about what you want to achieve in all the areas of your life.

Define Your Life Purpose

- What do you want to be known for?
- What is your purpose in life?
- Who do you want to be? Who do you care for?
- What do you want to achieve?
- What do you want to be number one in?
- What are you passionate about? What are you naturally good at?

- Which value do other people see in you now? What values do you want them to see?
- Who would care if you no longer existed? Who do you want to be a hero to?
- How do you want to come across to people? Which three words would they use to define you?

ACTION POINT: VISUALISE & DESIGN YOUR PERFECT LIFE'

Use the action sheet 'Visualise & Design Your Perfect Life' in the Playbook to define your life purpose and clarify what you want to achieve. An *audio version* of this exercise is available online to help you get in the zone.

Unless you are already crystal clear about who you are and how you add value to other people, do NOT skip this step. This will give you the opportunity to understand yourself at a much deeper level and help you document your self-discovery journey.

Note all the insights that come to you during this exercise. Do not make the mistake in thinking you will remember it all; you won't. Recording your thoughts enables you at the end of this process to trace your progress to see how far you've come.

Now, let's talk about your values and why this is important to understand.

What Are Your Values?

You should not start a business or a project without first figuring out what you want from that business or project and what are the most important aspects for you.

Most importantly, you should not get involved in a project that doesn't match your values. Don't make the mistake of saying you'll figure it out as you go because it'll be too late. Being clear about your values will avoid you wasting time doing something you shouldn't be doing in the first place.

You should live your values, embody them in your daily life and have the courage to stand up and defend what you believe in.

What Exactly is a Value and How Can You Determine Yours?

Simply put, our values express what is important to us. We all have a hierarchy of values which we evaluate against opportunities either consciously or unconsciously. What is most important for us comes at the top of the list and the least important at the bottom of the list.

What we pay attention to or what we focus on most in life is dictated by our values. How we spend our time and how we spend our money reveals our values!

SPOTLIGHT: Daniel Gurrola | The Inner Strength to Live Up to Your Values

"When you begin your career, you have a set of core values, and as you move along, a new set of values that are more consistent with your core values develop. But often you find yourself not having the inner strength to live up to those values and stand up for them.

"You simply go along, hoping they will never be challenged, and try to live according to those values. As you mature in life, gain more experience and become more confident in your own skin, you begin to really believe that these core values are an intrinsic part of who you are. That's what happened at my last job.

"At some point, I didn't believe the organisation's values, in particular, those of my manager weren't truly aligned with things I believed in and deemed to be right. It's around this time I decided that this organisation wasn't really for me. I wasn't thriving in this company and I was putting myself and the way I conducted myself at stake.

"I decided it was time to move on and when the decision came to move on, I embraced it. Today, I'm much selective about the organisations I talked to, and about the people I engage with and am willing to work for. **It's now a guiding light to the way I want to lead myself.**"

How to ensure you live according to your values?

"I think it's much more about maturity and self-confidence. It's a process, a journey to get there. When you start to see that you're not comfortable in certain situations, you begin to feel like you're not living your values.

"When you're being asked to do or say something not in line with what you believe in your core that's when you say, 'this isn't right.' This is not who I am, and I certainly don't want to be associated with this."

"Your values are your guiding light and influence your decisions in life."

Knowing your values helps you to understand what your brain focusses on, so you can be aware of how you make decisions.

Maslow's Theory of Needs

Abraham Maslow's Theory of Needs was significant for understanding human motivation. Further models have been developed to refine Maslow's work. But for our purpose, I'm not going to review all the models here. The idea is to understand we have a hierarchy of needs that explains why we do what we do.

According to Maslow, there is a hierarchy of five needs that we try to fulfil.

- Physiological needs: hunger, thirst, shelter, sex and other bodily needs
- Safety needs: security and protection from physical and emotional harm
- Belonging needs or social needs: affection, belonging, acceptance and friendship
- Esteem needs: worthy goals and ideals that give us meaning and purpose, self-respect, autonomy, achievement, status, recognition and attention
- Self-actualisation: personal fulfilment, growth, the drive to become our best self

The reality is people have different hierarchy of needs and do not necessarily follow the order described. This hierarchy was perhaps more in line with the thinking of the industrial age.

In today's world, some people would place a greater value in a sense of belonging and less on their physical needs, while others may be motivated by self-actualisation than focussing on a sense of belonging.

In the past, when people started their careers, they were more driven by the perks, financial packages, bonuses attached to a stable job that companies offered, and the need for security. As they moved up the career ladder, motivation shifted to more meaningful things, like connecting with others, and making a difference in their jobs and lives and leaving a legacy.

Today, young people want to change the world right from the very beginning. More and more millennials are asking for a meaningful company vision, corporate social responsibility and their contribution to society before the salary package. They want to buy into a company's mission and its greater purpose. They also tend to care less about owning a property, a car or other assets. Why buy anything when you can share it? This new mindset led to the success of the sharing economy, where people value more the usage than the property.

Additionally, more young people start their businesses straight after university and are happy to take risks rather than applying for a job that doesn't use their full potential.

The Six Core Values

Another interesting model that attempts to understand our human needs is the Six Core Values from the self-help guru, Anthony Robbins. He distinguishes six core values that most needs fall under: Certainty, variety (uncertainty), significance (status), connection (love), growth and contribution.

What we do often fall within one or more of these values. Listen[5] to his explanation.

Uncovering the Real Needs Behind Your Values

Sometimes, the value we claim to care about is not the real one. There may be hidden motives that are never uncovered. To avoid deluding ourselves, it's essential to uncover the real values we care about.

Your real need is the state you want, and the process to get there is only a vehicle.

Examples:

- Money is a vehicle for freedom. The real value is freedom.
- Wanting a family can be a vehicle for: contribution, love, connection (which are the real values)

To get to the core need or values, you can use the '5 whys' method. Take one of your values and test it.

Let's say you value volunteering.

- Why do you love volunteering? To help people in need.
- Why? To make them feel better.
- Why? So I can feel good, too.
- Why? To feel significant.
- Why? To be loved: Love is your real value!

Identify Your Conflicting Values

Sometimes, you can have conflicting values that sabotage what you really want. You want success, but perseverance is not on your value list. To take any consistent action, it's important to have values that are not in conflict; otherwise, you will never achieve your overall goal.

Where Do Our Values Come From? Understanding Mental Maps and Paradigms

Values come from episodes of pain and pleasure acquired throughout our life. We want to increase pleasure and move from pain, but this is largely unconscious. We often reproduce the same pattern of behaviour unconsciously.

Unless we stop and analyse our actions and recognise our patterns, we will never learn how to break free from them.

Understanding our mental maps and paradigms help us to recognise our patterns, and take that first step towards transformation. In my change leadership seminars and coaching sessions, I explain in depth this concept.

A paradigm is a model, a theory, a perception, an assumption or a frame of reference. It's the way we see the world, not in terms of the physical sense of sight, but in terms of perceiving, understanding, and interpreting. To understand paradigms, let's see them as maps.

But we know 'the map is not the territory' - Korzybski. It is just a representation of certain aspects of the territory and nothing more.

Imagine that you want to arrive at a specific location in Central London, let's say Hyde Park. A street map of London would help you reach your destination. Forget apps like Google Maps or Citymapper and assume your Smartphone has run out of battery. You only have a printed map.

Now suppose that there are printing errors and the map labelled 'London' is actually a map of 'Birmingham.' What are the chances of reaching your destination? Slim, I'll say. Can you imagine the frustration and the ineffectiveness of trying to reach your destination using the wrong map?

You may work on your behaviour: you can try harder, be more diligent, double your speed. But your efforts will only succeed to get you to the wrong place faster. You may work on your attitude and think more positively. You still wouldn't get to the right place. The point is you'd still be lost.

The truth is this has nothing to do with your behaviour or attitude; it has everything to do with you having the wrong map.

We all have maps in our head that we use to interpret what we experience. But we seldom question their accuracy and are unaware that we have them. We simply assume that the way we see things is the way they really are or the way they should be.

Two people can see the same thing, disagree and yet both are right. This is due to how powerfully our conditioning affects our perceptions and our paradigms. The way we think and see reality comes from the influences we had in our lives:

- Parents, family, siblings
- Teachers, school, church
- Role models, mentors, heroes, antiheroes
- Friends, work environment
- Goals you achieved or didn't
- Society in general, the real world with other people with different values

All of these people and events have made their silent and unconscious impact on us and shape our frame of reference, our worldview. Research has shown that these paradigms are the source of our attitudes and behaviours. We cannot act with integrity outside them. We can't be true to ourselves if we talk and walk differently than what we see internally.

Both our attitude and behaviour must be congruent with the way we see things. Thus, trying to change our attitude or behaviour is not going to work in the long term if we fail to examine the paradigms that led to those attitudes and behaviours.

Our paradigms also affect the way we interact with people. As clearly and objectively as we think we see things, we can realise that others may see them differently from our personal perspective.

"Where you stand depends on where you sit."

—Mile's Law

We see the world not as it is but as we are or as we are conditioned to see it. When we say something and other people disagree, we immediately think something is wrong with them. But as we can now understand, sincere, clearheaded people just see things differently, because everyone looks through their own unique lens of experience.

Our values, however, are not permanently established. We shift them constantly based on new information and from experience.

Understand therefore that other people may come from a different perspective and react differently to you while you are out there building your personal brand. There is nothing wrong with you if people do not agree with what you share. It's all about them and nothing about you.

Going back to our childhood, or from a time in our life when things were particularly difficult, can bring painful memories, but this is part of the journey. These memories provide clues into who we have become and give us the opportunity to liberate ourselves from our pasts. It also gives hope to other people who are going through the same experience and are willing to challenge the status quo.

Angela Levin,[6] a British journalist, revealed her *childhood experience* that included a tyrant mum who never allowed to be questioned. Angela became a journalist and writer who get answers to any question she wants. She also created a website *myhorridparent.com* to help children learn how to cope with a difficult parent.

This Pillar #1 gives you the freedom to be yourself. You don't need anyone's permission or validation to be who you want to be. It's time to create a new story, the story you want to live. Design your perfect life and live it right now. You have what it takes.

You only need to take this journey to rediscover who you are if needed. I reference several personality tests to help you discover further aspects of yourself.

Changing ourselves is more important than changing the world, but by changing ourselves we can change the world.

If recalling certain memories becomes unbearable, you may need to seek professional help and a therapy to sort out your issues. You deserve to be happy and it's never too late to start.

ACTION POINT: FIND YOUR VALUES

Use the action sheet 'How to Find Your Values' to identify them and change those that are holding you back or are no longer useful for your new goals in life.

What Is Your Mission?

You need to have a sense of meaning and happiness as you journey through life and unfold your passion. Even if you don't have the full picture, having a sense of where you're going will help you achieve more in life.

SPOTLIGHT: Sir Robin Saxby, Founding CEO and Chairman of ARM Holdings

Sir Robin Saxby is a fascinating leader who has a clear vision of what he wants to achieve at any time. This has been a key secret to his success in leading ARM to become the world's leading semiconductor intellectual property.

For him, it's essential to have a clear vision of the future, whether it's for the next twenty years, three years or twelve months.

Sir Robin started his first business venture at the age of thirteen when he set up a radio and TV repair business. His father recruited the customers and Sir Robin did the repairs. When they started ARM, Sir Robin and his team aimed to be the global standard IP, all with no pattern, no customers and no money.

But they spotted an opportunity[7] to focus on applications where ultra-low power consumption, high performance and low cost were critical, as well as positioned them as a force in mobile applications. They did a SWOT analysis to find their USP and didn't worry about things they couldn't fix.

What if you are struggling to create your vision? Observe the world around you to find people's frustrations and use your own experience, he recommends. Vision doesn't necessarily come from blue-sky thinking.

Sir Robin's mantra is: **Follow your passion, work hard and have fun.**

ACTION POINT: WRITE YOUR MISSION STATEMENT

Use the action sheet 'Write Your Mission Statement' to write what you want to achieve in life and how you want to express your values.

Profiling Tests

Sometimes it is difficult to be objective with ourselves, especially when we have been doing something that is not aligned with who we truly are for a very long time.

Taking a profiling test can give you useful insights that help you reconnect to your true self. You can find a lot of profiling tools online. The ones I've personally used and found insightful include:

• MBTI[8]

The Myers–Briggs Type Indicator® (MBTI®) is a profiling test that determines sixteen personality types based on our preferences in the way we construct our experiences. It uses a mix of eight elements:

  o Extroverted - Introverted
  o Sensing - Intuitive
  o Feeling -Thinking
  o Perceiving - Judging

My MBTI profile is ESFP: A combination of Extrovert, Sensing, Feeling and Perceiving.

ESFPs are good at many things, but thrive when in contact with people and having a lot of new experiences. They should seek careers that provide enough challenges to avoid getting bored. 8.5% of the total population is ESFP.

• Enneagram[9]

The Enneagram is a set of nine distinct personality types. The authors of the test explain that we emerge from childhood with one of the nine types dominating our personality with inborn temperament and other pre-natal factors. This innate orientation largely determines the ways in which we learn to adapt to our early childhood environment.[10]

My Enneagram type is a 7 with an 8 wing. Sevens are future oriented, generally convinced that something better is just around the corner. They are quick thinkers with a lot of energy and who make lots of plans. They tend to be extroverted, multi-talented, creative and open minded.

- Wealth Dynamics[11]

Wealth Dynamics is a personality test that tells you what strategy you should follow to build wealth. It is the world's leading profiling tool for entrepreneurs and reveals which of the eight wealth profiles is your natural path, giving you direction on what path to follow on your job, business and investments.

My Wealth Dynamics profile is Dealmaker with a secondary profile of Supporter. Dealmakers are naturally great communicators, influencers and negotiators. They have a great sense of timing. Examples of successful dealmakers are Donald Trump and Rupert Murdoch.

- Kolbe Test[12]

The Kolbe A™ Index is designed to measure the conative part of the mind — the actions you take that result from your natural instincts. The assessment validates your natural talents, the instinctive method of operation (MO) which enables you to be productive. Watch[13] a video with Kathy Kolbe, the creator of this test, explaining the science behind it.

My Kolbe profile shows a mode of operation as 4-4-9-2. The test indicates how we gather and share information (fact finder: explain), how we arrange and design things (follow thru: maintain), how we deal with risk and uncertainty (quick start: improvise) and how we handle space and tangibles (implementer: imagine). With a strong quick start, my natural advantage is 'Innovator'.

These tests reveal your strengths from different perspectives and uncover your natural abilities. Understand, however, that these profiling tests shouldn't limit whatever you can do if you assemble the right resources and go to work.

They have helped me to paint a clearer picture of myself and how to best pursue opportunities that are aligned with my natural talents.

Check the 'Resources' page to read how some entrepreneurs & experts, found their path.

Takeaways of Pillar #1 'Know Yourself'

The Pillar #1 is the foundation to build an authentic personal brand. You need to:

- Find your gifts and shoot for the moon
- Find what or who you care about and the cause you want to defend
- Identify what is important to you
- Embark on the journey of self-discovery
- Identify your values and the conflicting ones that sabotage your life
- Define your life purpose and your mission
- Take further profiling tests to better know yourself
- Complete the action sheets in the Playbook

Pillar #2 Master Your Expertise

'You can only walk in the shoe that fits you; nothing outside you will make you fulfilled'

Reading books, getting university degrees and attending lectures give you some of the knowledge you need in life and business, but the knowledge acquired can quickly become obsolete as the world moves at a rapid rate of change.

Gone are the times when you learned something in your degree, entered the job market and stayed there for all your life. Statistics show that the average person will make a career change 5-7 times during their working life. And the speed of change is increasing.

In today's digital age, knowledge is becoming a commodity, since it's readily available online. What we need is real expertise, preferably something that only you can offer because of our unique experience, insights, and background.

"Employers won't think in terms of employees – they'll think in terms of specialisms. Who do I need? And for how long?" —Julia Lindsay of iOpener Institute[14]

The truth is that without real expertise, no one cares about what you have to say. Influencers in the digital age are those that have a unique value that they provide, and that others care about. And it can be anything, as long as other people care about it.

To build a strong personal brand, you must provide something unique that others want, a tangible expertise, and continue to develop that expertise to stay relevant to your audience.

Pillar #2, Master Your Expertise, is all about that. You will have the opportunity to take inventory of your passions, interests and skills (PIS), learn how to transform them into a skilled, viable product or service that people want and will pay for.

Something that often puzzles me is when I see people who enjoy successful careers despite having poor grades at school while other people who graduated and have acquired many diplomas struggle to find their passion in life and get stuck in jobs that pay the bills, but they don't enjoy them.

Why is that? I think that the former were busy cultivating their passions at that early age that when they didn't 'fit' the education system, while the latter were busy learning to unlearn what made them unique and being formatted to think inside the box.

It's no wonder that after many years of conditioning, they can no longer figure out what their initial passion in life is, and they have to be willing to descend deep into the pit to find out where they left their passion behind decades ago!

What are Your Passions, Interests & Skills (PIS)?

Etymologically, passion means what you are willing to suffer from. It's an intense desire or enthusiasm for something, whether you get paid to do it or not.

An interest is an activity or subject that someone enjoys doing or studying. It doesn't matter whether you are good at it or not.

A skill is the ability to do something well; it's often learned or practised over time.

Never Take What You Know for Granted.

One day in my local library, I spotted a poster asking for volunteers to teach people IT skills. I started teaching there and saw how a life can be changed with the skills that I take for granted. One woman was able to attach her CV to an email and find a job, which had been eluding her for months, because didn't know how to perform this simple task. Another learner was able to create an email and book concerts places, something she had been unable to do. My oldest student was ninety-two years old.

Should You Follow Your Passion or Not?

There is a school of thought that encourages people to follow their passion, but another that says don't waste your time following your passion, do something that pays the bills or pick anything you want to achieve and figure out a way of doing it.

The fact is, most success stories were achieved by people who have a passion for something and the determination and obsession to pursue it. If they were not passionate they would not have put that much energy to achieve it in the first place. Those success stories include Bill Gates, Steve Jobs, Mark Zuckerberg, Elon Musk, Tony Robbins, etc.

However, other people found their fortune because they just started doing something and on their way, they find new opportunities, success, and finally their passion. Such stories include Dani Johnson, who started out as a cocktail waitress and made her way up, by learning how to sell and build a multi-million-dollar empire. Her passion to help other people get out of poverty and debt came later after she was able to achieve success for herself.

The point is that passion only is not enough. You need the ability to do the job and get the results that will lead you to your desired goals. This is the real distinction to have. We are all different. What works for you might not necessarily work for others.

STORY: Esther George | Passion for Computers Leading to Combat Cybercrime

Esther George is a cybersecurity and cybercrime prevention specialist. She works with international organisations, training prosecutors, judges and law enforcement how to deal with cybercrime. She is also the Global Prosecutor's E - Crime Network's (GPEN) lead cybercrime consultant.

"I became interested in computers and enrolled in a computer course, building and troubleshooting the old Amstrad 486s and Pentiums just before the year 2000. I realised how computers could be used for criminal purposes and decided I would devote my career to combating cybercrime, as it would later be called.

"I moved to the Crown Prosecution Service (CPS) HQ Casework Division and in 2002 the CPS established a High-Tech Crime Project, which I managed. I was tasked with raising CPS staff awareness of cybercrime and to train a cadre of CPS prosecutors to deal with cybercrime.

"I really loved my job at CPS. It gave me a lot of freedom that I built it to quite a good place until 2014. The problem sometimes is you can become a victim of your own success. I was given the mandate to train my colleagues, so we created a cybercrime solution that raised the profile of CPS employees as experts in cybercrime. My view was everyone should know about cybercrime at CPS, so we developed online courses and it was so well done that you almost didn't need to have a coordinator.

"I was asked to take on other work with some austerity measures coming in, so I knew I had to sit down and re-evaluated my situation. If I took on other work, at what point would I deskill myself in something I have been doing for so many years? I had to decide if I either wanted to deskill myself or stay in my niche. The final decision was to stay in my niche. The time had come for me to move on.

"Having a strong personal brand means you don't have to advertise or perform cold calls to get clients. A lot of people who approached me were either a current or former client. I even received recommendations from former colleagues."

Not everybody is lucky to be as clear about their passion, interests and skills as Esther is. In fact, most people struggle to boil down their passions, interests and skills (PIS). I call these kinds of people MIMEC™.

What If You are MIMEC™?

MIMEC™ stands for Multiple Interests, Multiple Expertise and Careers. Many people have trouble choosing one career; instead, they can navigate from one job to the next based on their ever-changing interests, curiosity and what they experience in life.

This is not wrong, like some people would make it sound and therefore portray you as indecisive and immature. It's just an insatiable curiosity and the ability to do whatever you put your mind to do. Rather than being condemned, I think it should be celebrated.

In her inspiring TED talk, Emilie Wapnick tells why some of us, who she calls 'multipotentialites,' don't have true callings.

An Explorer's Life

It's crystal clear now. Looking back at my experience and getting wisdom from self-reflection and a dozen of profiling tests, I understand the thread I've been following in life.

I had collected multiple degrees, diplomas and certificates across a variety of fields from information systems to finance and accountancy to consulting, coaching, journalism, marketing, etc. In all my jobs, I thrived the most when I was in a position to quickly start things and lead.

I talked myself into a job as head of the Information Systems department for a multinational oil and gas company at age twenty-four, and put in charge of running the mainframe of the company that I've never operated before. I was thrilled, a bit anxious, but I trusted my capacity to learn, which enabled me to hit the ground running.

After a couple of months shadowing the interim head and a week at an IBM centre, I was good to go. A few months later, I was leading a major network change to modernise the organisation's IT infrastructure. Two years into the job, the adrenaline I was running on was vanishing. I got into a routine and was mainly maintaining the systems, dealing with vendors and suppliers.

Then, an exciting development arrived. The company bought out a competitor and integrating the newly arrived information systems to the existing one added some fuel to my job. But shortly afterward the project was completed things went quiet again, but not for too long.

A few months after this first integration, unbelievable news broke out. The company acquired its biggest rival. Both multinationals had been competing for a long time. The fact that it was the less powerful company at the time that was acquiring the biggest was an additional reason to celebrate this event.

Things started to spice up again at work with gossip, speculations about how things will work out after the merger, which company will be the real boss, etc. Then one morning, my boss announced I would be leading the integration project for the merger of both systems. I was so excited, because I knew and respected the head of IT at the rival company, a mature and experienced man who had been with the company for many decades. And me, relatively new in the job with only three years in the company was chosen to lead this massive project.

That was one of the most exciting moments in my career. To take charge of it all. The task was big and with a lot at stake. Each day was different. I had to form my team, create sub-teams and appoint leaders to those sub-teams who would report to me and organise meetings, training sessions and report progress to my boss and to the headquarters.

Finally, eighteen months later, the integration of systems was a total success. I received the congratulations of the group project manager as one of the best-led projects of the group. I left the company a few months after that for my new challenge: complete a new degree in finance and accountancy in a year.

How to Create a Congruent Brand as a MIMEC™?

I am a self-confessed MIMEC™ unable to pick one thing and be content with it regardless of the promises I make that this will be the thing I will focus on going forward. I always failed after making such promises, because I find so many interesting things along the way that I want to know more about.

This tendency to switch from one subject to the next becomes a problem when you have to get on with a job that requires you to focus and master new skills. That's how I went through the process I describe below that explains how to get paid to learn all the time! Guess what? There are many job titles to choose from: journalist, writer, consultant, futurist and many more.

MIMEC™ people mainly seek freedom, connection and joyful experience in their jobs. Without those feeling they cannot experience true expansion.

One of the questions I'm asked often: How do you create a congruent brand if you are a MIMEC™? Isn't a brand one thing you should stick with all your life?

My answer is to be strategic about your condition once you diagnose yourself as a MIMEC™ and take the steps necessary to find how to make it your strength rather than your weakness.

Let me explain. If you are a business analyst in a bank and have two giant screens to stare at all day long while you're sitting at your desk on the 38th floor of an over air-conditioned building in some financial district and you are a MIMEC™, now is the time to do yourself a huge favour. Get out of there!

This is not the environment for a MIMEC™ who crave variety, human connection, movement and sensory stimulation. You got to decide as early as possible to live happily-ever-after and prioritise happiness over money. It's almost a matter of public health!

Okay. I know for some people this decision is not as easy to take on as it sounds. This is why you can take some time to plan your escape, and here is how:

Escape Plan for Trapped MIMEC™

If you have multiple passions and can't seem to know how to choose one, this section is for you. Do you remember going to a networking event and someone asked you the dreaded question, "So, what do you do?"

The classic answer of a lost **MIMEC™** is: "How much time you got?" LOL

I admit it has happened to me many times as I was exploring this, that and the other, all at the same time. I adapted my answer based on who I had in front of me. I could be, in turn, a trainer, a consultant, a journalist, a change consultant, a speaker, or a coach, whatever.

For someone with multiple passions, it's a struggle having to choose one thing, and I'm not asking you to choose one thing. Change your perspective instead and see it as having multiple strengths and passions. But only select one or two passions to create your brand; or even better, you can find a common thread to your main passions and create a unique package that only you have.

Most of what exist in life has two sides to it. The sweetest person can sometimes transform into a monster. A coin has two sides. There are good and bad, white and black, light and darkness.

What makes you think there is no other side of being a MIMEC™? Why beat yourself up because you can't seem to decide to settle on one skill?

Debbie Ford, an expert in the field of personal transformation and human potential, has worked on 'shadows.' She tells the story of realising that she was a bitch. Her first thought was to deny it, but the person who made her realise this asked her what was the positive side of being a bitch. After some thought she came up with a list of positive attributes and how it was okay sometimes to be bitchy. This changed her life! It is the exact same process I propose you should start now.

ACTION POINT: MIMEC™

1. List all the negative attributes you associate to being a MIMEC™
2. For each of them, find when it is great to have the opposite positive attribute

The irony is that it should be easy to define our uniqueness when we have multiple passions we can put together than being specialists of a single topic. But it's often the opposite that happens. And we are going to change that.

A lot of famous people we know, like Leonard de Vinci or Maya Angelou, had multiple passions. If you are fifty years old and still don't know what you want to do when you grow up, don't despair. Everyone is different. Some people know what they want to be at five years old. Others need more time to discover it. That's how it is and there is nothing you can change about it. This is also part of being **uniquely you.**

We are all on different paths. If you are someone who has been clear about your passion early on in life and followed it, congratulations. But if you are still looking for that one thing, there is no one thing! Stop and embrace all your gifts and make sense of them.

Embrace your 'flakes' and make your peace with the fact that you love all these eclectic disciplines. There is nothing wrong with you. It is strength and not a weakness if you use it strategically. Here is how:

- Know that not all of your gifts will or should make money. Not everything will translate in business. For example, I love cooking but that is not something I am willing to use in a money-making endeavour.

- Position them properly, frame them well and show how together they deliver a far greater experience for your desired market.

- Select what you communicate. Don't announce every new thing you get involved with. Wait until you get some tangible results and know you will be at it for a long time before you share it widely.

- Don't share unrelated experiences or skills that do not get you where you want to go

- Don't worry about what other people think. You will get stuck in any case, and not everyone will agree with you and your choice. It's your life, ultimately. Are you happy having many of these skills or are you looking to focus only on a few of them?

- Get someone to hold you accountable to your goals for at least 90 days and give them permission to challenge you.

The biggest challenge if you are a MIMEC™ is managing your time well. Be careful of not working without anything to show for it, because you enjoy it so much. Don't let a lack of clarity stop you from moving. It's time to take action.

ACTION POINT: 'FIND YOUR PASSION, INTERESTS & SKILLS (PIS)'

Complete the action sheet: 'Find Your Passion, Interests & Skills (PIS) in the Playbook. This exercise will really help you find clarity and picking a primary focus, whether you are a MIMEC™ or not. It is a process I personally used to focus on my current path without the sense of leaving something out

Now that you've picked your topic, you are ready to define what makes you unique.

What Makes You Unique? 6 Ways to Find Your Uniqueness.

Most people find it hard to answer this question; and me too. I've struggled with this one for a long time. But you can find the answer if you are willing to take a bit of time to do some soul-searching.

To answer the question 'what makes me unique,' whether you are looking for your next great job or you are a business owner, you need to know what other people are offering (i.e. your competition). You need to research your competitors and evaluate what they offer to see how you are different or see what they don't offer that can bridge the gap.

A solo consultant asked me once, 'How can I compete with McKinsey when I'm only a small consultancy?' My answer was, 'Don't compete with McKinsey.'

"Find out what is different about you and make it your competitive advantage."

The mistake most solo-preneurs or freelancers do is emulating an already established big company in the market. This is the quickest way to fail. There are 6 different ways to discover your uniqueness.

1. Your Life Experience

All the experience you have acquired up to now has been unique to you. Even if you are a twin with a similar upbringing, your life experience and how you approached it differs from anybody else's. No two people have the same life experience. This truth already gives you a point of differentiation in terms of the skills you have developed, and how your successes and failures have shaped you.

Write down:

- 5 moments of big successes in your life
- 5 moments of big failures
- 5 turning points when you have made a certain choice that could have been different
- What lessons you learned from these successes and failures

2. Who You Know

Who are the people you know because of your background, the work you do, where you live, most of your LinkedIn connections, etc.?

Write down at least 5 categories:

- Are they mostly affluent, executives, and high-flying people?
- Which industries are they in? Technology? Sales? Legal?

- Which profession? Are they accountants, lawyers, consultants, techies?

3. Your Original Viewpoint

It is not enough to know something these days. Anybody can Google to find any information, but having a distinction and a personal viewpoint on a topic is what people pay for.

Successful people create innovative business models based on a new perspective and a unique way of doing things. CNBC reported how Martin Roscheisen, the founder of *Diamond-Foundry*[15] came up with this idea after he sold his solar power company, Nanosolar. He and his team were looking where else solar power can make a difference. The diamond industry came to mind. But this industry has a decades-long history of human rights and labour issues, so Roscheisen said it was ripe for change. He figured out a new way to make high-quality diamonds in a lab in Santa Clara, California that are atomically identical to diamonds mined from the earth.

His new perspective on the diamond industry allowed him to create this new proposition based on his skills, background and new perspective.

You can find original viewpoints by considering these questions:

- What is your outlook in life?
- What do you hate or are frustrated with in the industry you are trying to fix?
- Which inefficiencies or injustice you are going after?
- What is your industry not doing or is scared of doing?
- How can things run more successfully?

- Which new ways do you see that can create more value to customers?
- How can you change the current rules of the game?

4. What is Your 'Big Why'?

Life can feel empty even if you have what is considered from anybody else's standard as a great life: kids, spouse, cars, and a good job. If you don't have anything outside of yourself that drives you to carry on no matter what, the time will come when you will feel a void.

This is what I call your 'Big Why,' your ultimate reason and what you are willing to die for.

Take some time to determine:

- Why do you do the things you do?
- What makes you get up in the morning excited and ready to start a new day?
- What drive you to do things you don't feel compelled to do otherwise? Is it for your family? Your kids? Your community? For a particular cause? For your nation?
- Let's imagine you've been given a magic wand that can only make <u>one wish</u> come true. Any wish, no matter how big or small. What will you ask? To cure all diseases on Earth? End homelessness? End wealth inequality?
- What are you willing to die for? Which cause will you fight hard to obtain?

It's this **'Big Why'** that connects you at a heart-level to your ideal customers and people who want to be associated with you. They buy into the big picture and what you stand for.

5. Your Pure Imagination

Create a totally new idea based on previously unrelated combinations, and from what people think is crazy or impossible, but you think is cool to do.

Elon Musk is one such people with crazy imagination, but also able to bring it to reality, like the electric cars with Tesla, or the Hyperloop transportation concept to connect distant cities in twenty minutes or less, or his other project SpaceX to make affordable travel space.

What are your crazy ideas?

Go for a walk in a quiet and inspiring place in the nature and let your imagination get wild. Write down the ideas that come to you.

6. Feedback from Others

If you don't have Elon Musk's fertile imagination, don't worry. All is not lost. You can ask people who know you well for feedback about how they see you and the best roles they see you in.

I've done this exercise many times with bosses, colleagues and clients, and the results can be amazing. This feedback sometimes uses the right words to describe us. Set up a survey with a few questions with Google Docs or Survey Monkey and send it to people you trust will give you honest feedback. If you don't like the feedback you collect or the answers don't really resonate with you, you can always discard them.

Take time now to go through these 6 ways to finding your uniqueness. It will pay off when the time comes to create powerful content with a unique perspective that your audience will love.

ACTION POINT: FIND YOUR UNIQUENESS

Complete the Action Sheet 'Find Your Uniqueness' in the Playbook

What is Your Value? Hint: It's in Your Positioning

Now that you have determined your uniqueness, how should you position and package that unique value, so people can see you as an asset and beneficial in solving their needs?

Your Bold Promise

What do you promise to deliver that is bold and exciting to your audience?

How will you ensure a consistent delivery on your promise?

Invest time to produce the results you want to be associated with for your personal brand.

Your Standard

Having goals you want to reach doesn't guarantee you will achieve them. Standard is what you settle for. If you want to reach your goals, you need to raise your standards.

Define the level you want to play at in life and at work. Some people are happy to play small when others think big.

You might spend as much energy trying to do small things or getting small contracts when you can get bigger ones and achieve more with almost the same efforts. It's up to you to decide which level you want to reach.

Would you rather spend one hour connecting to one high level client to get you £10,000 or would you rather spend the same hour talking to ten people to earn the same amount of money?

If you choose the first option, then you need to raise your standard to allow this to happen.

Which means you need to start being and feeling that way and go to places where people who are playing at that level are. You need to see the world through their lenses.

Some companies have high standards and excellent customer service.

Chick-fil-A's open statement says it all. 'We should be about more than just selling chicken. We should be a part of our customers' lives and the communities in which we serve.' Truett Cathy, founder

If you want to be successful and you are around unsuccessful friends, don't be surprised if you aren't making it. Be picky and know who is a user, a taker or a giver in your network.

Your standard applies to how you treat people too, including your staff, your clients, your suppliers, your family, and your friends. Do you treat them with the same respect or do you have double standards? Are you someone who encourage the best in people, provide constructive feedback, and offer help?

How you choose to position yourself will determine who you attract. This leads us to our audience and people we want to serve. Position yourself and your business powerfully to make a difference.

WHAT ARE THE KEY SKILLS TO DEVELOP FOR THE DIGITAL AGE?

"Any kind of job is going to have a digital component. It doesn't mean everyone's got to be a computer scientist." —Satya Nadella, CEO of Microsoft.

Developing partnerships & relationships

"In addition to having some technical skills, the entire digital age is about ecosystems. An ecosystem means lots of players involved in developing a product, a platform or a service. When you have lots of people involved, this also means partnership. But at the core of this idea is openness, the ability to be open and to work in multi-interest and multilateral situations. This is where relationship building plays a very significant role.

"First you need to understand that in the digital age it's more about ecosystem and less about single products.

"The second thing you need to understand is about openness, reaching out to others to join this, understanding what you bring to the party and what others bring too, but being very realistic about what every party brings to it and what every party wants to get out of it. That again requires relationship building skills.

"The third is about coming together for a common purpose and delivering something that is unique and compelling either for a business, a consumer, an end consumer or an institution, but delivering something compelling to them in a way that it wouldn't have been possible by a single body or person or institution. It is really the ecosystem that brings a compelling proposition to others." —Daniel Gurrola

Searching and multiple perspective thinking

"You need to develop research skills, not Google-ing things. Google is a company. You need to know how to search on Google, Bing, Yahoo, etc.

"Know how to use <u>Boolean</u>, basic coding skills, not so much advanced skills like cloud based integration, so when something breaks you know the basics to fix it.

"Develop your ability to detect fake news. You must have the ability to understand larger issues and context, and be able to think more strategically. Right now, people are very tactical. They want to see the short term and are not looking at the long term. They're not looking at all the factors and forces that go into something. They are much segmented, including in their thinking. You can be segmented, but you need to have the ability to put it all together, because a lot of people think through one lens.

"Develop multiple perspective thinking. We are more global in the way we live, what we eat, what we buy, and where we get our food from. Everything we do is global. So, people have to understand those aspects. People say I don't want to be involved in that country, meanwhile you're getting your cabbage or vegetables from that country. We need to be aware of that." —Suki Fuller

Ability to keep up on what matters

"Know your terrain. As technology happens in a blink, you have to keep up but keep up only if it's relevant and has meaning to your purpose and to your skill set. So know your terrain – know what's out there.

"Choose the digital strategy that is going to help your personal brand and master it. Once you can do it with your eyes closed, choose another if you feel like it and master it too, but keep on up-skilling yourself so you never fall behind." —Naomi Sesay

Check the 'Resources' page to read how entrepreneurs & experts found their strengths.

Takeaways Pillar #2 'Master Your Expertise'

- Find your Passions, Interests and Skills (PIS)
- What to do if you are a MIMEC™ (Some with Multiple Interests Multiple Expertise and Careers)?
- Six ways to find your uniqueness: your life experience, who you know, your original viewpoint, your big 'why,' your imagination and feedback from others
- Define your value with your standard and a bold promise
- Complete the action sheets in the Playbook

Now that you have defined your strengths and your unique talent and expertise, you need to know who can benefit from what you've got to offer. This leads us to Pillar #3, which demands to be clear about who you want to serve, which will be your desired audience.

Pillar #3 Know Your Audience

"Marketing yourself means you talk to your audience and get to know them very well."

Trust is the most valuable currency in the digital age. You need to establish trust with your desired audience. But with the fragmentation of the marketplace and its fierce competition, it pays to pinpoint exactly who you are serving.

Are you passionate about working mums, business executives, or human resource professionals trying to retain their talent?

EXPERT TIP: Don't Assume! Study Customer Interactions and Behaviour | Riaz Kanani

Riaz's earlier years in business taught him a useful lesson: it doesn't matter how cool your solution is. If your customer doesn't understand what it will do for them, you will not succeed.

"We founded Digital Oxygen in 2000. At the time, the use of video was extremely fragmented and difficult to use. What we offered was an easier way for our customers to use technology that worked for different types of computers. We naively thought we would easily win business, because we were three times better than the nearest competition, which meant anyone making money through video would make money three times more with our solution, so how possibly could they not buy this new technology?

"It didn't happen. It turns out technology can be scary to people when the company is new and the programming they offer hasn't been accepted as the standard. So, we changed our business model to aim toward video advertising rather than a licensing business, as we intended. When we did that our objectives were easier understood by potential customers. Business took off and we were able to expand and grow very quickly.

"I study how consumers interact and exhibit behaviour on the Internet. Businesses must understand this as well and analyse their data. This got me interested in working with companies to help them better understand their customers.

"Every company needs to either make more money or reduce costs. Marketing is often seen incorrectly as being a luxury expense. Making sure you generate revenue and find efficient ways to do it is going to be important.

"To get your audience's attention, you need to offer something of value. To influence them, you've got to say something worth paying attention to. So just talking to them in a social context isn't going to be enough. You need to show you are moving something forward or you're adding value to them."

You cannot be all things to everyone and not everybody will like you. Being selective when choosing your audience allows you to get a deeper understanding of their issues and pick the problems you are most passionate about solving.

Let's start the search.

1. Soul-Searching: Who is Your Ideal Audience?

• Who do you want to be a hero to?

Focus to determine who they are and how to bring them more energy, more enthusiasm, and more excitement. But it needs to be mutual. They need to lift and charge you up as well. If you're working with clients or other people that drain your time and energy without offering much in return, it's time to find a new audience.

I want to be a hero to driven people who are looking to make a big impact in the world. Those that are self-centred and only obsessed with how much money they can make for themselves are not people I enjoy working with.

• What do they do?

What are their biggest problems? Understand their problems and how you can solve them, and how to engage with them successfully online.

If they have distinct problems/needs, you may need to segment them into separate groups with the same problems to solve. Segmenting customers into homogenous groups with similar preoccupation and outlook on life will help you to communicate more powerfully.

Let's say you are passionate to serve executives, but you can further slice this population down. Are they CEO, CFO, CMO or HR? Beyond the fact they are all in the C-suite, these populations have specific needs and problems to solve. Your communication will be more specific and engaging if you communicate directly to their needs rather than having a generic and broader communication.

For that you need to create different personas that represent each category of your audience.

2. Determine Your Ideal Customer Avatar or Customer Persona

Start to determine people who are most likely to value your service and are willing to pay for what you are offering. Being selective allows you to make a bigger impact more quickly. Find your early adopters.

A **persona** represents a complete picture of a category of your buyers. You group your clients into categories by using defined criteria that are common to them.

- Define the demographics: age, profession, sex, affluent, CSP+, etc.

- Psychographics: find out their pain points, needs, interests, goals, desires and motivations; what keeps them awake at night! Understand your audience inside and out, and what is happening in their world. Ask them, but don't stick only with that information. Look for what they search for online, what they read, and which TV programmes they watch.

- Anticipate their needs by examining upcoming trends that can provide them an awesome experience.

- Which problem are you solving among all of their other needs? Select the ones they are willing to pay you to solve. Is it a big enough problem? Are there many people who have the same problem? If not, no problem = no business.

CASE STUDY: Customer Persona, Becky

Demographics: Becky is a single 40 y.o. consultant and trainer who has freelanced for approximately ten years.

Psychographics: She used to consult for a corporate company, but is finding her current contracts a bit boring these days and not very exciting, She relies too much on the few companies that employ her, and faces constant, unfair 'company' politics.

Her dreams: Becky wants to reinvent herself and get to the next level in her professional life to grow her business, to be able to choose clients she would be excited to work with, and make a difference in their lives.

She wants to succeed, but no longer wants to compromise on who she is and what is important to her.

She also wants to stop trading time for money by leveraging digital technologies while having more time to enjoy her personal life.

Her needs: But there is a problem. Becky has no clue where to start this soul searching and is not very confident how to use the Internet to build and grow her business. She uses Facebook, LinkedIn and Twitter as a contact management system to add work contacts and people she meets at networking events. But that's all. She knows she could be using the same digital networks as a strategic-led generation system to raise her profile. She is also unsure how to position herself in a unique way to stand out from the crowd.

Now that I understand Becky's needs, interests and goals, I can design a solution that will address her challenges, as well as those of hundreds of other people who are in a similar situation. This is a customer-centred approach rather than thinking about what you have and how to sell it to potential clients.

Although the persona created is based on an ideal person that may or may not exist, with their particular needs, desire and wants, many other people will identify with Becky and resonate with this description during your promotion.

You can create as many personas as you want for your business to group people with the same needs. This helps you to serve them better. Having your persona in mind when you communicate will be specific and vivid in a way that a generic publicity cannot match.

3. What Your Ideal Customer Persona Searches Online?

When you start your search, you don't know for sure what people are searching online. You need to make a few assumptions of what your ideal persona could be searching to solve their problems/needs.

Look at the words they use in online groups on LinkedIn, Facebook, and other forums that describe their needs. Collect some information with a survey, if you have a list, to find out more about their needs. Ask people you know that are in your target group.

Once you have an idea of the words they are using, check them with *Google Adwords* or *SEM Rush* to see how popular those keywords are.

Keywords are very important in the online world. Using keywords that people are searching enables you to be discovered by your desired audience. It's also by using the right keywords that you will be able to do a Search Engine Optimisation (SEO) well. This is an iterative process. You may not find the right keywords straight away; keep looking for alternative words people use to find your type of information.

ACTION POINT: CREATE CUSTOMER PERSONA

Complete the action sheet 'Create Your Customer Persona' in the Playbook.

4. Does Your Audience Know They Have a Problem?

Entrepreneurs sometimes see a problem that their prospect doesn't recognise yet.

- Find out what your customer wants.
- Tell your customer what problem they have and how you are solving it for them.
- Describe which process you take people through to achieve their goals. Even better, <u>show</u> them.
- Create easy to remember frameworks to explain your processes. Name your frameworks and services with memorable and copyrightable names, such as MIMEC™
- How current are you? It doesn't matter if you used to be an expert twenty years ago. How relevant is your knowledge today that conveys to your audience you can help solve their problem?

5. Show How You Care About Them

Your audience needs to see that you care about them before they care about you. Never forget: It's all about them.

1. Find out what they want and give it to them.
2. Explain the value you will provide them specifically in such a way that you are seen as the obvious choice.
3. Ensure that your audience understands why the problem you solve is relevant and meaningful to them by spelling out clearly the benefits. Don't make the mistake of assuming they already understand them. Articulate those benefits clearly and how their lives will be much easier after adopting your solution.

4. Make sure your audience can see you as a credible source for their solution, and that it can help people like them by sharing your story and how you helped others in a well-orchestrated campaign. We will cover this in further detail in Pillar #6, 'Connect with Empathy.'

If you can accomplish these four things, you will develop a powerful connection with your customer, and quickly become a recognised expert to that group of people.

Building and reaping the benefit of a strong personal brand doesn't happen overnight. To become more influential, listen carefully to your audience and build a product they truly want.

People buy from people they know, like and trust, even in B2B settings. I have never seen a tower or a building come to buy something. They will buy only because they believe your solution is better than what they currently have.

Check the 'Resources' page to read how entrepreneurs & experts understand their audience.

Takeaways of Pillar #3 'Know Your Audience'

- Determine your ideal audience, define a customer avatar or customer persona
- Find out what your ideal customer persona is searching online
- Detect your audience's problems and pinpoint them if the customer is unaware of them
- Show you care about them before they care about you

Pillar #4 Lead Your Niche

"If people don't tell you you're crazy, you're probably not doing something that will change the world." —Jacqueline Novogratz, Acumen

To lead your niche you must develop the ability to see what others don't see and execute it perfectly. It comes by observing how the market you want to play in is evolving, but also what is going on in other sectors.

What Is a Niche & Why Pick One?

Niche etymologically comes from French dating from early 17th century. Literally it means 'recess' from the word nicher, 'make a nest.'

Nowadays it denotes or relates to products, services, or interests that appeal to a specific section of the population who has a problem or a need they are willing to solve.

With today's fierce competition and the fragmentation of the marketplace, it's impossible to be good at many things and talk to everybody effectively at the same time; therefore, it makes sense to choose a positioning that appeals to you and the audience you want to serve. By focussing on a smaller portion of the market you can quickly understand what makes a winning proposition and get quick feedback rather than trying to be too broad.

When I started my business, I used to think it was limited to niche down for fear of losing potential customers. I was wrong, as I found out the hard way! Not selecting a clear niche is hard work with very limited results. Your voice gets lost amongst thousands of louder ones. Being selective allows you to make a bigger impact quickly. Some topics, however, are already specialised and don't require much to niche further down, like speed-reading. But even then, one could argue that having a segmented approach to it like speed-reading for students or speed-reading for busy executives can be more effective to communicate the specific benefits to each of those segments.

How to Select Your Niche?

There are many ways to niche down. You can target a specific occupation, industry, gender, generation, geography or special life stages.

A Niche = Your Topic + Something Specific

Let's say your generic topic is high performance. To niche down, you can add one or many specifics:

- Occupation: High performance for engineers (1 level)
- Industry: High performance for engineers in automobile (2 levels)
- Gender: High performance for women engineers (2 levels)
- Generation: High performance for millennial women engineers (3 levels)
- Geography: High performance for millennial women engineers in emerging economies (4 levels)
- Life stage: High performance for millennial women engineers in emerging economies after a baby (5 levels)

The further you niche down, the more likely you are in being the expert who leads in that niche.

Of course, you can think about many other ways you can niche down. The sky is the limit of what you can come up with.

You can find unique niches by combining your life and professional experiences into something unique. Pay attention around you. Observe what's going on in your environment or in new places or when you travel. Sometimes ideas come in the most awkward ways and as a result of something you've been struggling with for years.

Chandler Bolt, the founder of Self-Publishing School, a platform that helps authors write and self-publish their books, tells his story of struggling with writing for many years.

Despite that he managed to become a best-selling author and created a business to help other struggling authors. Chandler's example shows that sometimes our challenges can be where our biggest breakthrough comes from.

Before choosing your niche, it's worth doing a reality check to find out if that niche is profitable enough. Just because you like a niche doesn't mean people will pay you for it.

Is Your Niche Profitable?

The best niches are those with hungry customers with a huge sense of urgency and are willing to pay for it.

The Boston Consulting Group's (BCG) matrix, routinely used in management, can help determine how profitable your niche is likely to be.

+ Unique product/service −	Hobby (2)	Desirable (4)
	Find a job (3)	Price (1)

− Value to the Customer +

The vertical axis indicates your ability to provide a unique product or service and the horizontal axis the value of that product or service perceived by the customer.

- The first corner is where you create something of great value to the customer, but other companies also offer that. In that corner, you compete on price. You can still make money there, but it is always about price.

- The second corner is where you create something totally unique but of no real value to the customer. In that corner you just have an expensive hobby. This is where you find some of the inventors featured in Dragon's Den, the UK TV show that keeps inventing new products without caring if there's a market for it.

- If you provide something that is not unique and is of very little value to the client, you'd better find a job.

- The corner you are supposed to end up in is at the **top and to the right** where the customer has a great need of your product and service and you have a unique ability to provide it.

'**Must have**' solutions are so much more compelling than '**nice to have**' solutions. If you can't put your hand on your heart and say, 'If I was the customer, it would be a no-brainer,' then you need to change or improve your product/service, or reconsider your desired audience.

Is Your Offering Sustainable?

A profitable niche is good, but you should check if the problem you want to solve is a big one. If the number of people who have this problem is huge and growing, this is a good sign.

It's easy to be seduced by 'an idea' or 'a scientific breakthrough' or 'a cool technology' that has no proven customer demand. You also need to check if people are willing to pay for your solution by voting with their wallet. Do a small test where you ask people to pay and see what happens.

How to Position as a Premium Brand?

In a world where most things tend to be commoditised or free, creating a premium brand is one of the smartest strategies business owners and professionals should consider. Here are seven ideas to consider:

1. Be the only source of your expertise by choosing the right niche.

2. Charge for value. Do not compete on price. Low price is not a sustainable proposition as a cheaper competitor will always come along. This means you need to sell to value-conscious people and not price-conscious ones.

3. The 'who' is very important in your success. Don't try to sell to people who don't have money to buy or are cheap genetically. Some people are fundamentally stingy and always ask for free stuff or discounts. I know a lifestyle concierge company owner who

struggled for years to recruit new clients, but once she switched and positioned her service as luxury concierge, the business picked up multiple times.

4. Understand your audience very well and delight them. They will be grateful for it.

5. You can't provide a great experience on the cheap. Disney, Lego and other luxury brands provide an experience that a low cost won't. Easy Jet is a no-frills airline company that gets you from a point A to B, but you do not expect anything more. On the other hand, La Compagnie is an exclusive business class only airline that operates flights between Paris and New York and promises customers to deliver an awesome experience in human-sized planes at an affordable cost.

6. Don't be afraid of polarising people. Create product or service that some people love and other people hate. Many people try to create a product or service that is perfect for all age groups, all genders, all religions, all everything, and they end up creating nothing worth remembering.

7. Don't be scared to invest in acquiring great leads. Figure how much it costs and include it in your price. Think in terms of lifetime value (i.e. the total amount a client is likely to invest with you).

Your Unique Selling Proposition (USP)

What is the solution that solves your audience's problem better than anyone else's? This is your unique selling proposition (USP)

Which problem do you solve and how?

Among the needs identified for your niche, select which specific problem you are uniquely placed to solve and tell how you go about solving it.

Let's go back to Becky, our Avatar. Her problem: She wants to build her consultancy, working with people she likes and stop trading time for money. The solution:

• Define what makes her unique

Define her **unique value** by looking at her experience, what she likes, her passion, what she spends most of her time doing (even when she is not paid), and who she loves helping, etc.

I will also help her to unlock her internal conflicts to understand what is holding her back in expressing her gifts and what she believes in. What often prevents people to stand out as we've seen earlier, are their beliefs and fears.

Using Pillar #1Know Yourself and Pillar #2 Know your Expertise, I can help Becky explore her identity and uncover what drives her to make a difference in her business.

• Build the Business Positioning

Next, Becky will use Pillar #3 Know your Audience to define who her ideal customer persona is, and Pillar #4 Dominate your Niche to determine her unique positioning.

Later, we will create a communication plan to connect with her audience. She also wants to gain time back and stop trading time for money. I will show her how to create a smart suite of products in the Pillar #6 from a one-time delivery and how to create recurring income that doesn't require her to be physically present to deliver great value to her audience.

Digital assets are great to generate money automatically whilst she sleeps or when she's on vacation. If she is sick and can't deliver her services in person, no problem; the automated online shop will keep making money.

How to Create a Killer Unique Selling Proposition (USP)

In this section, you will brainstorm ideas to find your USP and put these ideas together in a message for your audience by using the step-by step method below:

Step 1: Determine the Biggest Benefits of Your Product/Service

Clearly describe the **5 biggest benefits** of owning your product or customer experiences with your service. What value are you adding to clients?

Your prospect doesn't care if you offer the best quality, service or price. You have to explain exactly WHY this is important to them. Think in terms of what your business does for your customer and the end-results they desire from a product or service like yours.

James Saward-Anderson, founder and director of The Social Selling Company, explains they are targeted and focussed on getting ROI rather than building endless strategies. They apply sales in a social context to deliver results to small business clients who don't have a sales team.

Step 2: Brainstorm What Makes Your Offer Unique

Your Unique Selling Proposition (USP) separates you from the competition. Your offer should identify what needs are going **unfulfilled** within your industry or your local market. The need or 'gap' that exists between the current situation and the desired objectives of your customers. Businesses that base their USP on industry performance gaps are successful.

Find out what are the most frustrating things your customer experiences when working with you or your industry in general.

Alleviate that PAIN in your USP and make sure you can deliver on your promise. Brainstorm what makes your offer unique by considering one of the 12 areas below. Think outside the box and ask feedback from clients.

1. Quality

Is your product/service of a superior quality compared to your competition? What exactly? Is it the content, where it's produced, venue or the materials provided?

Chick-fil-A® promise customers great-tasting, high quality fast-food with products made with fresh, simple ingredients right from the kitchen.

2. Service

Do you provide exceptional customer service?

Zappos.com, the online shoe and clothing shop, promises a quick delivery with the best service.

3. Delivery

Do you deliver on the promise and beyond your promise? How?

Uber's promise is one tap and a car comes directly to you with no reservation required.

4. Speed

How fast do you execute your services, act on an enquiry, bookings, complaints, etc?

Domino's Pizza uses 'Pizza delivered in 30 minutes or it's free' USP to become wildly successful. This worked because of the need or 'gap' in the market. After a long day at work, Mom and Dad are too tired to cook, but the kids are starving and don't want to wait an hour! They want pizza NOW.

5. Convenience

How convenient is your service or product? Do you have favourable opening hours? Do you plan your schedule to fit your clients' needs? Do you provide different ways of accessing your product or service?

Deliveroo promises 'takeaway delivery from premium restaurants near you.' You no longer have to eat only pizza if you want food delivered to your home.

6. Experience

Great experience matters. Take the service to spectacle. Connect emotionally. Include drama, tell stories, and provide a great customer experience. How amazing is the experience you provide to your clients? Do they leave you happy and fully energized? Do you provide them undivided attention?

Walt Disney World promises to 'create a magical holiday for your family.'

7. Price

Unless you are a low-cost service provider, cost shouldn't be part of your USP. You cannot compete on price forever. A cheaper newcomer will slash the price even further to get you out of the business.

8. Heritage

If you have established your business a long time ago, or have inherited your skills from a long tradition, you can use your heritage as a key differentiator, explaining the beginnings, the key achievements, transitions, prestige, recognitions, etc.

The iconic London department store, Selfridges, has a long history which started in 1906. The founder, Harry Gordon Selfridge, arrived in London from Chicago to open his dream store based on his revolutionary understanding of publicity and the theatre of retail. This spirit of innovation and creativity is still present today.[16]

9. Who you serve

Who are the people you serve? What is their status, hierarchical position, role, industry, size of company, generation, etc? Are they mostly affluent executives or high-flying people? Are they in technology? Sales? Are they accountants? Lawyers? Consultants?

10. Your unique framework, methodologies & viewpoint

What proprietary tools have you developed that help your clients to achieve their goal faster and better than your competition? Do you have a different way of solving problems in your industry? It should be articulated so customers clearly see the benefit.

The YEANICC™ framework I have developed to build a personal brand is a proprietary tool that set me apart from other people who haven't developed their own methodology.

11. Your imagination

You can create a strong USP based on your own imagination or by linking previous unrelated fields to create your own universe. Think outside the box and what could be possible.

12. Scarcity

Scarcity drives desire and economics. You can choose to work only with a finite number of people/ businesses and create scarcity for your offer. Exclusive clubs use this technique to create desire and have a long waiting list of hungry people waiting to pay a high fee for admission.

You can work with ten clients per year and give them your full attention for a premium price or you can chase one-hundred low paying clients not very committed who need a lot of support. Which category would you pick?

What then if prospects must prove to you why they should be accepted as your clients? They not only have to pay premium fees but also need to be committed to do whatever it takes for their success.

The Genius Network, ran by Joe Polish, is a network where members pay $25k to join but also has to meet stringent selection criteria.

Your client success is your success. The more success you can create for your clients the more they will advocate for you and the more you can use them as a case study to attract even more high-paying clients.

Step 3: Be Specific, Offer Proof & Guarantee

• Testimonials

Consumers are sceptical of advertising claims companies make. So, alleviate their scepticism by being specific and offering proof when possible. Provide past client testimonials that show what you have been able to achieve for them or use your own example if you embody the proof of your offer.

• Guarantee

Think about it. What really bugs your customers? Get into their shoes, then consider them saying this, 'If I could just find a [business type] that did [x], I'd deal with them every time and recommend all my friends too.' Think of all the big frustrations of your customers. For each of them develop a guarantee based on them.

The basic format for a powerful guarantee is simple. 'If this doesn't happen, then we'll do that.'

Example: If you take the personal branding course, you watch the videos, do the exercises and find you are not getting a greater clarity about yourself within 30 days, ask for your money back with no questions asked or hard feelings.

Step 4: Write Your USP

Use the relevant items you've listed earlier to complete this section. Write your USP so it creates desire and urgency.

1. **Catch Your Customer's Attention**

- WIIFM: what's in it for me? Tell the customer how your offer will benefit him. Use the benefits listed in step 1.

- WSGAI: what's so great about it? Tell the customer why your solution is important to them in a way they feel compelled to pay attention.

2. **Condense into one clear and concise sentence**

The most powerful USPs are so perfectly written, you cannot change or move even a single word. After you get your USP written, your advertising and marketing copy will practically write itself! Now take all the details about your product/service/offer from the steps above and sculpt them into one clear and concise sentence with compelling and vivid words. Write your draft now.

Step 5: Tagline Development

In this step, craft a tagline or a slogan for your offer. Successful slogans are concise, simple, have a double meaning, are keywords, etc. It doesn't need to be a grammatically correct sentence, just something snappy and unambiguous.

Examples:
- Just do it: Nike
- Think different: Apple
- I'm worth it: L'Oreal
- Every little helps: Tesco

CASE STUDY: Milena Bottero | From Struggling Intern to Founder of a Home-Sharing Platform, *Room for Tea*

Milena Bottero graduated in environmental policy from LSE and did an internship after her studies. When she finished, the only job she could find was another internship, then another and most positions were unpaid.

"I didn't think it was fair and I figured out that if I wasn't going to be paid, I'd rather do my own thing, so I created my own job.

"It was almost accidental. I experienced a need and saw other people around me experiencing that same need and I decided to set it up as a project to see where it goes. We got so much demand that it picked up very quickly, so I just carried on."

Room for Tea (RTF) was born during a hackathon day in 2011. Milena found the name 'home sharing' boring and brainstormed with other people to come up with RFT that they found cool. Creating the 30-second pitch was also a team effort. Each member of the team wrote their version, then compare and discussed them. There has been much iteration since the first version. "Room for Tea is a **peer to peer** accommodation platform **matching hosts and guests** globally for **mid-term** stays."

What makes a good pitch according to Milena? The pitch should flow and everyone in the team should know it by heart, she says. And they have different versions, tailored to who they're talking to: investors, guests, hosts or the general community.

A longer version of the USP for the community is "RTF adapts the concept of homestay to serve a generation of young professionals who want to live and work in different cities around the world."

They wanted to highlight that they are building a global movement.

The benefits that each side of their clients get are clearly defined and communicated by using impactful keywords.

Benefits for the hosts
1. Find a guest you can trust
2. Earn some extra cash without feeling like you are running an hotel
3. Enjoy experience but not long-term commitments
4. Support from RTF throughout the process

Benefits for the guests
1. Experience real life in a shared home
2. Safety: verified hosts
3. Fair pricing
4. Meet someone like-minded (they can meet and discuss before the stay)

They want to make it affordable for anyone, but the platform is a marketplace. Hosts want to make money but are prepared to offer a lower rate due to the safety element and they want someone who is a real part of the house, not someone who wants to be in a hotel.

Having a strong brand has enabled Milena to inspire trust, get people interested in using the service and get free press in national newspapers. So far, the company has grown organically by word of mouth and social media, and with a few online ads. But RTF is looking to run events in the future to enable guests and hosts to meet and include an 'ambassador model' to grow rapidly.

Determining your USP is the first step in dominating your niche. But, you also need to understand the landscape of the marketplace, the terrain you want to play in and how to position against other players.

Understand Your Marketplace

"Prepared leaders stand ready to meet the future."
—John C. Maxwell

Analyse Your Marketplace and Key Trends

What are the key trends driving your industry/field? The marketplace follows the same cycles and seasons in life. Learning to recognise those cycles and seasons is a key skill in building a successful business and stay ahead of the competition.

New trends come and go, but your ability to determine if the market is in an ascending or descending phase is crucial.

Just like the seasons, there is a moment when a new trend starts, like spring, then matures into summer where the sales happen. It then moves into autumn where consolidation happens with mergers and acquisitions before entering the winter phase where systems and processes make it easier to replicate the business. And it's time to start again with fresher insights.

A smart woman that understands the seasons is Oprah Winfrey. She left cable network at the height of her fame to set up her OWN online channel. Most people didn't understand that move but this bet on the future is proving fruitful.

Each season has its own rules that you need to respect. There is a time for everything and you need to take that into consideration. On the one hand, it may be more difficult to enter a saturated market unless you bring in a clear differentiation or innovation. On the other hand, there is no point trying to consolidate an industry that hasn't reached maturity yet and is at a budding stage.

You need to check:

- Where the industry is at in its maturity level?
- What is the market size? Is it growing or decreasing?

If you are in a business that is thriving, it's maybe difficult to recognise the adequate moment to switch and move into a new business to take advantage of emerging trends. The start is often patchy, messy, sometimes with a lot of bugs and the quality not yet maximal. And the market leaders often think their customers won't accept the change or aren't ready for it. Kodak infamously failed to adopt digital cameras. Motorola dragged its feet on developing a digital phone. This allowed Nokia to lead the way. Blockbuster and Blackberry, who once dominated their markets, are now relegated in the shadow.

When you think about it, it seems normal when everything is going well for your business, you don't need to change what you are doing, but history is full of examples that show what a fatal mistake this can be.

No success lasts forever and the time to change is when you are doing well. Do not delude yourself, and be willing to face the brutal reality and change when the time comes, or history will just repeat.

To anticipate and prepare for the turn of events, you need to dedicate time in spotting weak signals:

- Monitor trends to spot weak signals. Observe changing customers' behaviours and how technological, political, social, environmental, legal and economic factors influence your market place.

- What everybody in your field is talking about?
- What used to be valued in your market, but is no longer relevant?

Understand Your Competition

Who else is serving your niche? Identify the key players, what they are offering, and find the gap to emphasise your differentiation point.

- Who are the major players? Select the top 5-10 businesses that are offering a similar product or service as you. Find how they create value and how they promote themselves. Learn what makes them great and model them whilst keeping your own originality.
- Who are the latest entrants or challengers?
- Find the gap! Where in the ecosystem can you be best placed? What is it the other players don't offer that you can add to your offer to stand out and be different from those you've studied?

Creating Your Own Rules of The Game

What would you rather do if you have the choice? Play by the rules of others or play a game you created with your own rules?

When you create your own rules, there is no competition and it's more fun and profitable.

But how do you create your own rules of the game? There are many ways:

1. Disrupt the Way Things Work in Your Industry

Interrupt usual habits. What are you frustrated with in your industry? What your industry is not doing or is scared of doing?

Imagine having to commute daily and facing long driving queues sometimes as long as 210 km. You lose many hours daily to the congestion and wish you could get to work or meetings faster. This is the ordeal that people face daily in San Paulo, Brazil. Voom was born. A platform backed by Airbus where you can book a helicopter to skip the queue at a 'reasonable price.' They pool helicopters available in the region on their platform using the same model as Uber.

Instead of suffering hours in a traffic jam, busy executives can now get to work or meetings in fewer than ten minutes. Urban helicopter taxi service becomes a reality for congested cities. And as demand grows, the price will keep falling, enabling more people to use this service.

This is an example of what can be done to solve some of the biggest challenges faced by a sector.

You can add new services or instead reduce the services offered to simplify the complexity if needed.

2. Create an Ecosystem

What constitutes your core value? The content you provide or the network around?

In a connected world, the ecosystem you create around your products or services is one of the most valuable assets to have.

Businesses that are moving to digital platforms realise they no longer are in the business of selling products or services. They are in the business of creating a connected ecosystem of offers, all of which work together to solve the user's pain point. In the past, these companies would have solved that pain by creating a product or service for customers, but today they create a **whole ecosystem** of connected offers via a single platform.

On that platform, there are various applications and it is open to third parties to create even more apps to add more value. The more apps you have, the more jobs you can get done for your customers.

This is what the big digital players have done:

- Apple with iPhone, iTunes, iPad
- Amazon with books, shops, films, music
- Facebook with a multitude of apps for users to do more than basic communication with friends
- Android with millions of apps that are available to run on the platform
- The new arrival Echo, by Amazon, where Alexa, a voice-command assistant executes a range of actions based on skills developed by a multitude of third-party developers

Nike is evolving from the business of selling shoes to creating a whole ecosystem of connected offers with its apps (including the Nike+ Run Club) to create a community of runners, all of which interact with each other and help to solve the user's pain point in a much larger context.

The company may continue selling shoes, but the shoe now sits within a larger ecosystem of offers that together create value for the users.

Any company that can engage its users in a connected ecosystem and attract third parties to create a thriving ecosystem of value exchange has a strong chance of getting ahead.

The books *"Platform Revolution"* and *"The Digital Transformation Playbook"* explain in great detail how to build such digital platforms.

3. Disrupt an Incumbent

Pick an industry or a sector. Find out which inefficiencies annoy customers the most and how to create new value, not just by moving online what is done offline, but create a new type of value that didn't exist previously.

WeWork is an example of a company that has disrupted the office space rental to compete with commercial real estate. The company rents empty space from landlords and transforms it into shared workspaces and rents them out to individuals and small businesses at a fraction of the excruciating price that traditional office space rent used to propose. [17]

Udacity is another example of disruption in the education space. Unlike other e-Learning platforms, which offer courses across a wide variety of topics, the platform focusses on tech and teaching specific skills technology employers are looking for. The company partners with leading Silicon Valley companies to create and tailor courses, or what the company calls 'nanodegrees.' These courses cost $199 per month across 6-12 months versus a course that cost $6000 per year or more.

If you limit the new service to do online exactly what is done offline, the incumbents with their financial power and market reach will be able to fight back by creating a similar platform. You must offer something that the incumbents cannot offer to disrupt their business model.

How to Stay Ahead of the Curve?

It can seem overwhelming to stay relevant in your field with so much moving so fast. To stay focussed on your goal you need to have a system in place to collect, then keep up only on what matters.

- Set up a Google alert for keywords that interest you.
- Listen to conversations on social media by following relevant hashtags.
- Subscribe to relevant newsletters, using a dedicated email address.
- Read industry publications and look outside your sector. Disruption often comes from outside the sector, so pay attention to what is going on inside and outside your field and keep up with new developments.

Check the 'Resources' page to read how entrepreneurs & experts lead and stay relevant in their field.

Takeaways of Pillar #4 'Lead Your Niche'

- Why you should pick a niche
- Select a profitable one
- Why position as a premium brand
- Create a killer unique selling proposition
- Understand your marketplace and key trends that are driving your industry/field
- Understand your competition, but also create your own rules of the game
- How to stay ahead of the curve

Pillar #5 Control Your Image

"You can't maintain fake for too long!" —Suki Fuller

We've all heard the expression 'don't judge a book by its cover,' but with millions of books published today, when a reader browses for books, whether it's on Amazon or in bookstores, the cover is the main factor they will pick a book. The book cover design industry is thriving. So, image matters.

Image branding is what some people have in mind when they think about personal branding. Image is important but can't fulfil its full promise without the foundation from the other pillars.

You need to take control of your image. Just because you want to develop an authentic brand doesn't mean you should be sloppy, especially if you are positioning as a professional brand.

It's not about being a fashion victim, but your physical appearance and visuals should tell a story and reinforce the message of the other elements that you send out.

I am not a fashion victim. In fact, I will share a secret with you. I used to be a tomboy! Anything like manicured nails, make-up, perfectly plucked eyes brows, etc, for me is an utter and total waste of time. But I understand that to project a professional image, a minimum of grooming is necessary. So, I really do the minimum I can get away with.

1. Define Your Personal Image

You need to define how you want people to perceive you.

- Is your style relaxed with T-shirt and jeans like Marc Zuckerberg from Facebook?
- Is it chic and glamorous like an Yves St Laurent model?
- Is it conservative or classic like Jackie Kennedy?
- Or is it trendy or eccentric like Lady Gaga?

Choose the style that suits you and project the values that are important to you. Express your personality and preferences.

Mari Smith, the Facebook expert, is known for her turquoise colour, whilst *Joe Pullizzi*, the founder of Content Marketing Institute, always wears something orange. *Seth Godin*, a marketing expert and bestselling author, has perfected his futuristic look with his big yellow glasses.

ACTION POINT: EXPRESS YOUR IMAGE

Refer to the action sheet 'Find Your Values' to pick the values you want to express visually in your image.

Taking care of your physical appearance goes a long way towards your success. Look your best at all times. You can get an image consultant professional advice.

You need a professional photo on all your online presence, and preferably the same one. Your image is even more important to define if you create videos, as you will need to project your personality that sets you apart from the rest.

Check the 'video branding master class', nucleusofchange.com/training-video-branding where I provide step-by-step training to define your identity and present with authority.

Since this book is about building a personal brand to advance your business goals, let me give you an overview on how to build your business image just before we get to the action point.

2. Define Your Business Image

The image of your business embodies all the qualities, the feel and values you want to reflect inside and outside the organisation. Your business image or visual branding is what people see first and how your business is recognised. Think about the golden arch of McDonald, the tick symbol of Nike, the apple sign for Apple. Those are visual representations that also create the identity of these businesses.

The Elements of Visual Branding

Logo

A logo is a visual representation of your company and tells a story by itself. It can be a symbol, an animal, an abstract concept, an object, etc. The sky and your imagination are the limits.

Sometimes, instead of having a single logo, if you have distinct departments in your business or distinct lines of products or services, it makes sense to create a family of logos that have the same feel but with their own individual identity.

An entrepreneur that does that well is Roger Hamilton[18] with his range of products and services: Wealth dynamics, Talent dynamics, Entrepreneurs' institute, Entrepreneurs resorts, etc. You can recognise them to be part of the same group, using the same colour but different shapes and having their own individuality.

Another way of representing a family of logo is to have the same generic name and add a different word like Virgin group.[19]

To create a professional logo, you have many options. Check *99designs.com*, *peopleperhour.com*, *fiverr.com* or ask your friends.

If you know about design, you can create your own logo using professional software like Adobe's Photoshop or Illustrator. Alternatively, if you just need something quick for a prototype, you can buy a ready made logo you can personalise by using *canva.com* or *themeforest.net*.

Colours

Another important element of the visual branding is colour. You need to choose a palette of colour that best represents what you do and your company personality and use it across all your marketing materials.

Each colour evokes a different emotion:

- Red is often associated with energy, power, passion
- Gold often symbolises the feeling of prestige, illumination, wisdom, high quality
- Blue is the colour of the sky and sea and often symbolises trust, loyalty, confidence

Find out more about colour signification at *color-wheel-pro.com/color-meaning.html*

My dominant colour is gold, as you can see with my different logos on my website francinebeleyi.com/products.

nucleus of change *Francine Beleyi*

That is because I want to express the vibrancy and warmth of my personality.

When choosing many different colours, make sure they go well together. You can check how to create complementary colours at *color.adobe.com*.

Typeface and Fonts

You also need to choose a typeface that best represents your company personality.

A typeface is the design for a set of characters. Popular typefaces include Times Roman and Arial. The typeface represents one aspect of a font. The font also includes other characteristics such as size (10pt or 12pt), weight, italics, etc.

The main types of typeface are Sans serif and Serif. The former uses small decorative lines while the latter is composed of simple lines. As it shows here, Arial is sans serif and Times New Roman is serif.

Choosing one typeface versus another depends on many factors. Ilene Strizver, the founder of Type Studio, has a useful post[20] to help choose the right font for your brand.

You can also ask a designer to help you choose the most appropriate typeface and design brand guidelines that will work best for you.

Your Tone of Voice

How do you want to communicate to your audience? Which language do you want to use? Do you want to be formal like the BBC? Informal like Proper Corn? Authoritative like the Financial Times? Fun like Innocent Drinks? Playful like Mailchimp? Inspiring like Tony Robins? Challenging like Seth Godin?

Define how you want to sound to your audience. The words you use will convey the tone of voice that fits your personality. Ensure you communicate in this manner across your marketing ventures so people recognise your authentic voice straight away.

Check the 'Resources' page to read how entrepreneurs & experts manage their image and reputation.

Takeaways Pillar #5 'Control your Image'

- Define your personal image with your unique style that projects your values
- Choose a unique logo or a family of logos
- Choose your colour, typeface and fonts
- Define your tone of voice

Pillar #6 Connect with Empathy

"Make your message impossible to misunderstand."
—Nina 4 Airbnb

Building an influential personal brand is a long-term commitment. So, providing well thought out and quality content frequently and across a variety of channels is necessary. It doesn't mean that your content should be complicated, but you need to learn simple strategies to amplify your communication.

Tell them your story, your struggles, as well as your successes. Don't try to portray yourself as someone you're not. Communicate who you are genuinely but as a leader, you should also think about the impact of your communication on others and promote a positive agenda.

"The critical issue is to be confident that the knowledge is being used wisely, in other words it's in the long-term interests of all the stakeholders."

—Prof Bruce Lloyd

1. What is the Best Way to Communicate with Your Audience?

You may be hearing that video is an important medium now, but you hate seeing yourself on camera. Are you a wordsmith instead or would you rather talk than write?

Some people are **Visuals.** They prefer seeing things. Others are **Auditory.** They learn best when hearing things out. And others are more **Kinaesthetic** and prefer having an experience. They'd rather do things, and learn best that way.

Having your preferred way of communication is one thing. But does your ideal audience also like to consume content through that medium? They might have a different way of absorbing information and learning.

Although it will be easier to start with the medium you are most comfortable with, the most effective medium will be the one your audience prefer. If you love video, but your audience prefer reading, you'd better provide a transcription of your video to maximise your reach and engagement.

So, before you choose a communication channel, observe the way your audience consume information and survey them.

To reach a wider audience, produce the same content in different modalities:

- **By speaking**: audiobook, podcast, videos, speaking from stage, webinars, etc.
- **By writing**: website, blog, e-book, book, whitepapers, etc.
- **By experience**: videos, speaking from a stage, webinars, seminars, etc.

It can be tempting to use many mediums when you start to maximise your reach, but this strategy can be time consuming. It's best to pick one or a maximum of two to start with before adding others.

Once you've picked your preferred medium, study the top people who are crushing it in that space and learn from them. Sign up to their newsletter to receive their communications and look on their social media channels.

How Experts Use Media

Video: Marie Forleo and Brendon Burchard mainly use videos to build their authoritative content.

Audio: John Lee Dumas from Eofire primarily uses daily podcasts to connect with his audience. Jo Polish and Dean Jackson also used the 'I Love Marketing podcast' to spread their wisdom.

Writing: Carol Tice from 'Make a Living Writing' primarily uses blogging to get known. Dorie Clark writes for Harvard Business Review, Forbes and other authoritative publications to establish her brand.

The best way to reach a wide range of people is using multimedia content with a blend of written words, figures and engaging visuals using original images, fonts, graphs, info graphics, colour, etc.

2. Make Your Original Voice Heard

To build an influential brand, you need to share your perspective, how you think things should be, and express your view point with no ambiguity. The work you've done in Pillar #2will help you here.

When you hear someone speak at a conference, when you read a book, or listen to the news, what is your take on what you've heard? Do you agree or disagree with their views? Do you think there is a nuance to bring to what they say?

Jot down your thoughts and rephrase what has been said. It will become your perspective.

Originality is what people are looking for, not rehashing and saying what everybody else is saying.

Review the Action Point **'Find Your Uniqueness'** in the playbook to refine your perspective, if need be.

3. Storytelling: Tell Inspiring Stories that Connect with Your Audience

How You Became Who You Are?

We, humans, are social animals who want emotion and to feel connected. Stories inspire us, encourage us, and challenge us to think about something we have not considered before. It gives us hope that change can happen despite the odds if we take one course of action over another.

It makes people feel connected to what is presented at a heart level, not an intellectual one.

Being able to tell compelling stories about you and your solution and connect to your audience is the fastest way to inspire people to take the action you want them to take.

Another reason you should tell stories is most people don't remember facts or hard-core evidence, but they keep in mind vivid stories. Think about the last time you heard a presentation. What do you remember from the talk? The statistics are a story you connected with.

To build an influential personal brand you need to **tell stories.**

Select an experience that shaped you—your key defining moments and struggles that can explain how you have finally come to the solution you are presenting. You can also tell the story of the future that can be created with help from the audience.

All great leaders are excellent storytellers, and are able to sell us a future that is not yet there.

The famous 'I Have a Dream' speech is such an example. Martin Luther King Jr. described a vivid and inspiring future that people wanted to see fulfilled.

Another master storyteller was Steve Jobs who managed with his keynote speeches – translate commercials – to create anticipation and desire from raving fans and people who couldn't wait to hand over their money in exchange for his products.

The charity sector is also very good at telling stories, because it moves people to take action by tapping into their emotions.

Create a Library of Personal Stories

Your story is not told in a vacuum. It should support a message you have for a specific audience, which can be your customers, potential investors, future recruits, or attendees of a seminar, or your personalised keynote.

Your goal might be to teach a lesson, inform or inspire your audience to change their perspective or behaviour. Choosing a personal story that best support your message's goal can make a big impact. You need to create a library of stories for you to use when it's necessary.

To find gripping stories, look back on your life. Review previous action points to identify critical moments you can use to support your message for more impact. Some of the best stories can be found in:

- **Your childhood**: what you remember that shaped the way you think or behave today
- **As a teenager**: the challenges you had to overcome at home, with your friends, at school, your successes, the transitions you went through, key lessons you've

learned, vivid moments that shaped you with teachers, family, travels

- **As an adult:** your first job pleasures and pain, flying solo from the family nest, your colleagues, your bosses, how you loved or hated a job, what you discovered about your strengths and in which circumstances, what broke your heart or made you proud, how you overcame challenges or led successful, key projects, who was there for you or not, what key lessons you've learned

Pay special attention to **transition times** when you move from one place to the next, how you adapt, who you met along the way, and who helped or were obstacles to your progress? Which jobs you liked and those you hated and why? Which frustrations or discouragements you had throughout your journey to success?

Don't tell long stories, but focus on **key moments** and explain what made you take one course of action instead of another and the role they played in your current path.

One Key Moment

After my A level, I enrolled in medical school and wanted to become a medical doctor. Then I had my first computer class. The teacher, a geek looking man who studied in Russia, explained how the future will look with computers that will process information faster, and how we will be sitting in our room, ordering food, and other futuristic ideas. I was hooked. I wanted to be part of that future. I left medical school and enrol for a computer science degree. I didn't regret that move.

Create a Memorable Story

Telling a compelling story about you and your solution is the fastest way to get your audience to take the action you want them to take. You need to be the hero who has braced adversities to get where you are. Here are steps to create a powerful authority story.

- What are your audience's top aspirations or dreams related to your solution?
- What are their top fears and frustrations?
- Why did you decide to create the solution? What was your motivation?
- How did you manage to find or create solutions to their needs?
- Which struggles did you face along the way to get to this result? (these struggles need to be similar to theirs)
- Present your solution and the benefits they will get once they've used it
- Finish with a call to action, what you want them to do

STORY: Building a Platform for Travellers, with a Difference

Audience's aspirations: They want to travel in a new country and be able to live like a local without feeling like a tourist

Fears/frustrations: Their experience in a new country is often inauthentic and they end up doing the tourists stuff without seeing the real country. The bespoke solutions are always too expensive.

Why: John wants to make travelling cheaper to travellers and have a personalised experience as well as generating jobs to the young, local population who are often unemployed.

How: He was a tour guide in the past and became frustrated with seeing the same spots proposed to tourists and not the real experience of the country. He thinks there's a win-win proposition to get young locals involved, to build friendship with tourists, and show originals spots whilst making money.

What: He created an online platform that easily and safely connects local personal tour guides to earn money, and travellers who save money whilst having a personalised experience.

Call to action: Want to join a trusted community to show you original places in your next destination? YES

Often people do the opposite. They start by telling you what they sell and why it's so awesome, without building the case for it. This approach is not empowering at all.

Don't worry if your story is not perfect the first-time round. Keep improving it again and again until you are totally satisfied. But don't delay sharing it.

5 Tips to Make Your Story More Impactful

- Go straight to the point to grab people's attention in the first seconds.
- Tell the story with vivid words and specific details without being too long. Use metaphors, symbols, and myths.
- Have a clear beginning, middle and end.
- Add elements of a roller coaster to keep people engaged. Build tension with a clear conflict that

climaxes at the end with resolution when the person changes.

- Have three versions of a story: 90 seconds, 3 minutes and 5 minutes

To build your storytelling skills further, read the fairy tales you loved when you were younger. Look at the structure used in building the story. Watch your preferred films critically by analysing the structures used in trials and tribulations.

ACTION POINT: CREATE YOUR LIBRARY OF STORIES

Use the related action sheet in the playbook to create your library of stories that you will use in your messages consistently.

4. The Power of Conversation

The paradox is that the digital age enables more connections between people but the art of having conversation seems to get lost. People have more friends, more followers and more fans but there is a very short attention span and the quantity is impacting the quality of conversations. It's important to have meaningful conversation with your audience and other stakeholders to go beyond the superficial and co-create the future.

"After studying strategy for many years, I have come to the conclusion that the quality of decision-making depends more on the quality of conversations about issues related to the decision than on anything else." —Dr Bruce Lloyd

"When you start talking to people, you start in your comfort zone and talk to people you know, people you trust. Along that journey, they will introduce you to their friends. Check what their perspectives are, where they are coming from, what's going on in their world, and then, frankly, it is about the conversation you have. Be open and always make it an exchange and not a one-way street.

"Be prepared to be vulnerable, but also listen to others and empathise with their vulnerabilities as well. Those things can go a long way." —Daniel Gurrola

"To build meaningful connections, especially if you're doing it in for business, follow up. Be authentic and when people respond, follow up, have a conversation. We've lost the art of having conversations, because social media is such a short span attention channel you think you are having a conversation. No, it's not. That's your initiation, not your conversation.

"Once you start having a conversation with someone they're going to ask questions. Be interested. Ask questions back. It's not about you. At the end of the day it's about them. So, keep on asking questions. 'Tell me what else you want me to do? How can I help you?' That's how you continue connecting, by having conversations." —Naomi Sesay

5. Create Digital Assets that Attract Your Desired Audience

To get your desired audience to come back again and again, you need to create conditions to attract them and build an inspiring ecosystem that keeps them engaged. This means you need to establish your authority and build a library of digital assets that you will use to demonstrate your expertise and thought leadership.

We will cover this in greater details in different chapters. Key digital assets include:

Website

As someone who needs to be visible online, you need a website with a 'yourname.com' URL and another URL with your 'companyname.com' and other URLs for your products and specific landing pages.

CASE STUDY: How I use my Websites

My personal website francinebeleyi.com is where I feature all aspects of my public profile in general. It includes the links of all my other websites including my blog.

My product sites nucleusofchange.com and mydigitalpal.com are dedicated to my business and what I offer. The first site is about my consultancy services and the latter is where I teach various topics on how to thrive in the digital age. Perrsonalbrandinginthedigitalage.com is dedicated to this book and all the related materials and services.

Each site has specific landing pages that are used for specific promotions and only that. There is nothing else on those pages. They can be used to offer a free resource, promote a new product, an event a webinar, etc. An example of landing page is mydigitalpal.com/egrow2017.

Blog

A blog is where you showcase your expertise and use as a central hub for your content.

Business blogging leads to 55% more website visitors according to <u>Hubspot</u>. Blogging can serve many functions. It's a place where you share your knowledge and showcase your expertise at length. It enables you to test the popularity of your topic, as you get immediate feedback from reader comments. It's a great way to learn more from customers and create products and service that best serve their needs. You have, however, the possibility to disable comments if you do not wish to collect them.

Blogging is an opportunity to educate people further on your products and services without being sales-y. They can see a different side of your business and you can be more casual by sharing behind-the-scenes images or videos they won't see on your official site.

You can use your blog to also build your list by having an opt-in form to collect readers name and email addresses in exchange for a free report, info-graphics or further tips that solve their problems. At the end of each post, you can add a call to action, which directs readers to a specific landing page where they get something related to what they've read.

A blog attracts potential customers and partners.

Blogging helps to communicate your ideas clearly and with more impact. As you go through the learning curve, you become a better communicator.

You can use written words or video, which is called vlogging.

A blog can be turned into a book, using the most popular posts and comments from readers. It can be a self-published book or a deal that a publisher offers because of the audience you attract.

Some blogs are money-making machines and their primary function is selling by educating readers how to make better choices and directing them to buy on Amazon, Shopify or other merchant sites. It can lead to many affiliates opportunities, partnership or sponsorship offers and to create products and services, membership sites, etc.

If you started blogging on something you are passionate about, it can be transformed into a business if it becomes popular and the demand is there.

Another benefit is if what you write is searchable on Google. Writing your blog content with SEO in mind and using the right keywords will create traffic to your site as people search for those keywords and land on your blog, offering new leads.

Ultimately, you gain influence with a blog that becomes popular and valuable. It helps people who find it valuable and trust you. You become an expert in your field and build a strong personal brand.

EXPERT TIP: Blog to Connect With Your Audience | Olivier Zara

Olivier Zara is a management and social media consultant, blogger and author of 7 books. He has been creating content for more than fifteen years and has developed a system to create content fast for his blogs and his books.

He uses Post-it notes to jot down ideas as they come, and always has a stack of them close by. When he has enough material, he groups the Post-it into themes and looks at them critically to determine what new thinking he is bringing to the topic.

Olivier's specialist blogs on Collective Intelligence and Personal Branding are a good way to test ideas and topics that people love. He adds his unique perspective to the themes and writes a blog post. He then looks at reader comments and uses the most popular posts to write a book that include additional elements.

"You don't want to write a book only with the compilation of your blog posts, even if they are super-popular," he says. "It doesn't add extra value to your regular fans."

His strategy is to run separate blogs with specific themes rather than having a single blog that regroups them all. This separation enables each blog to rank higher on search pages for the theme, and attracts the right audience. But it also means having to work harder to keep all the content fresh.

For him, the only time it's okay to have an all-in-one blog is when you are starting out and haven't yet figured out the direction of your expertise. Once you are clear and want to use your blog to advance your position as a thought-leader in your field, a dedicated blog with an overarching theme is advisable.

His motto is **one theme and three rules**: quality, quality and quality. Quality is more important than quantity. Olivier would rather take the necessary time to develop thoughtful content and posts once a month if he has nothing to stay.

"Do not get into the trap of posting at all cost, but keep a good rhythm that allows you to produce quality content with the resources you have," he advises.

Email

Your professional email should be with your domain name and not a Gmail or Yahoo email address. It's an ideal medium to use to promote what you do by inserting your e-signature at the bottom of emails with the links to your products and services.

You should also collect emails from your website and other channels. This is what is called 'list building,' a key to building further relationships with people who are interested in what you offer. Building or growing your email list is crucial for email marketing and in sending personalised offers to your audience.

For more information on email marketing, check the resource page.

Social Media

You need to be on relevant social media sites. It's where your audience is. Have your profiles fully completed. We will see in a while how to choose the right site channels for your brand.

Videos

Producing weekly or monthly series of videos where you share 'how to' tips or interviews of experts in your field are great in building your authority in your field.

Check my master class, nucleusofchange.com/training-video-branding for more information about using videos.

Podcasts

A podcast is an edited piece of audio content that you can listen to online or download as an mp3 file. It is often available for free or with a paid subscription that automatically downloads new episodes to your computer, mobile application, or portable media player.

You can produce podcasts on a specific topic or theme with daily, weekly or monthly episodes and you can host them on iTunes, Stitcher or SoundCloud with links to your website.

Podcasts are great for educating an audience on a specific topic, but it's also a great lead generation tactic.

Eofire.com is a popular podcast where John-Lee Dumas chats with inspiring entrepreneurs 7-days a week.

Book and e-Books

There is something magical about books that propel you as an expert faster than other assets. I cover this more in depth later in the book.

E-Courses

E-Learning is now a trillion-dollar economy. People need to update their skills fast, on the go and on demand to keep up with the changing world. Many platforms sell e-Courses. The production of the course can be done cheaply and fast. It's also a great way to introduce people to your work and get new clients for your business.

Media kit

You should have a media kit available for journalists, the press, bloggers, and for people who want to feature your story on their platform. A media kit includes high and low-resolution photos, a biography, your business profile, success stories, case studies, and anything worth talking about.

Speaker's profile

If you want to be booked for speaking engagements, industry conferences, keynote speeches, you need to have a one-page speaker profile available electronically with high-res professional photos and a speaker's show reel that event planners can consult with.

Other Digital Assets include Apps and Assessment tools

These digital assets can be built easily today to connect with your audience and make money whilst you sleep. With the availability of the digital tools, you don't have to be a geek to put this together. In the next chapters, I will cover how to orchestrate the distribution of your assets to get the most out of them.

6. How to Choose Your Main Social Network Channels?

The famous marketing phrase, 'Location, location, location' still applies. In a brick and mortar world, the success of businesses depends largely on where the business is located. A busy location where a lot of the right customers pass through is more likely to provide you great results than a dead-end road where a few people venture.

To build a recognised personal brand, it's important to be in the right place, and on the right social media sites that your customers visit.

However, it can be overwhelming to think about all the social media platforms that are available and deciding which you should invest your time in. Don't try to figure out what is the latest tool on the market, but instead focus on what is going to move the needle for you to build your personal brand.

How you choose which medium to focus on depend on where your audience is and which network will maximise your return on investment. Don't overstretch yourself or try to be everywhere at the same time, spreading yourself too thin.

Be primarily on the channel where your desired tribe is and you feel comfortable using. Do not force yourself to be on a channel that does not fit your personality, especially when you start. Pick a channel where you can resonate with people.

If you come from a corporate background and Facebook and Instagram seem alien to you, start with LinkedIn where you will find the same codes you are familiar with. On the other hand, if you are a fun-loving person, and much of a creative person, you might want to try Instagram or Facebook first to get your feet wet. When you understand the benefits each channel provides, you can make an informed decision and add extra channels for increased visibility.

Different Levels of Connections: Suki Fuller

"**Facebook** is like my house where I only let a close group of friends and family in. People who are entrusted can come in.

"**Twitter** is like my front lawn or a back garden. You can come into my garden or into my front lawn and on my porch, and occasionally you might say something I might not like. That's why you're not in my house. You could have a different opinion or be completely annoying. Occasionally, you might do something that my neighbours don't like. I can pretty much tell you, 'OK. Get off my lawn,' then shut the gate and you're not allowed to come back. You might be on the other side and still lob a lot of stuff over, once in a while.

"**LinkedIn** is my office. This is where I put my professional connections. You can say things at work you wouldn't say at my house. You can have your opinion and you're entitled to it, but at work you maintain a level of professionalism."

Don't mix up the different levels and know how to use each of these channels effectively.

The fundamental issue today is how to communicate your message with different types of audiences across different distribution channels and stay consistent.

Dr Dambisa Moyo, an influencer on LinkedIn with 900k+ followers, is a global economist and author who recognises that tailoring her message to different channels to touch different generations is a struggle.

During a CBNC Life Hacks Facebook live session, I asked her to share some tips in building a strong personal brand today.

'You have to be able to discuss your view with many different audiences,' she says.

In the past, traditional media was a key component in building a personal brand and there was only one way to put your message forward, but today she says this is very different. "You have to tailor your message to each channel whilst maintaining your focus on the key deliverable – your message – without losing credibility."

Focus on the main social media channels

There are hundreds of platforms and social media channels today that are likely to evolve. In this book, I only focus on the most used social media in terms of population for the last four years.

LINKEDIN

LinkedIn is a social networking service for businesses and professionals. The site is available in over 200 countries worldwide in 20 different languages and had 467 million members in the third quarter of 2016.[21]

I joined LinkedIn in 2005 and was part of the first million people on the network. Back then, it was mainly a network to find CEOs and recruiters to connect with. Today, 466 million people later, the platform has evolved. But it's primarily mission[22] remains the same.

As a professional, you should be on LinkedIn to make better use of your professional network to grow it by linking with other professionals, generate leads, and get noticed by recruiters and potential clients. It's also a great medium to stay informed with news in your field, posts, specialist groups, and even learn new skills with Lynda.com, the e-Learning platform, now integrated within LinkedIn

This network enables you to find people across industries and functions, to share insights and news, and to build your brand as an expert in your field. It all starts with having an all-star profile and a title that tells clearly who you are and what you do.

People who are on LinkedIn are serious about business. This is one of the few platforms where it's okay to be blunt about your business.

Check out 'How to Create a powerful LinkedIn Presence' at mydigitalpal.com.

TWITTER

As of the second quarter of 2017, the micro blogging service has an average of 328 million monthly active users[23].

The 140-character platform enables to communicate your ideas succinctly. But the enriched multimedia feature that includes photos and videos allows you to communicate much more.

One of the key features of the network, the hashtag, helps others find all information grouped under that topic or word. These hashtags are used for various purposes: to talk about products, companies, a particular topic, a cause, etc.

Popular or trending hashtags bring awareness of the causes behind them.

Michelle Obama supported the #Bringbackourgirlshashtag when young girls were abducted in Nigeria by Boko Haram. Rebecca Enongchong, a tech entrepreneur campaigned with #Bringbackourinternet to get the government of Cameroun to reinstate Internet connections they cut.

Twitter has an open-door policy and allows users to anonymously share their views and thoughts on the network, encouraging trolls, which can have a repulsive effect on some users.

On the other hand, you can connect easily and quickly with influential people in your industry by following them and linking with them when the opportunity arises.

To find experts in a certain topic, search the corresponding hashtag, then see which individuals or companies share the most relevant information. Create a list and add all the relevant Twitter accounts inside the list.

You may for example create a list called Innovation. Search #Innovation to display everyone that share information with this hashtag. Select those who appear to be real experts in innovation to add to your list.

You can also keep abreast of what is going on by following trending hashtags on your Twitter home.

BuzzSumo helps to analyse what content performs best for any topic across multiple platforms. You can see how many times a post or tweet has been shared.

Tweet Deck is a tool that allows you to stay in touch with what's happening now.

You can also use your own hashtags to build your personal brand. They can be a topic that your audience search for or a made-up hashtag you use personally when you publish information.

Periscope is a live video streaming app. Although it belongs to Twitter, the app has its own identity. In 2017, the live streaming network counted 1.9 million daily active users[24].

The app is popular with journalists, politicians, travellers, businesses showing behind-the-scenes video, demo products, entertainment, sharing 'how-to' live videos, and anyone who wants to stream their events.

YOUTUBE

YouTube[25] has over a billion users–almost a third of all people on the Internet–and every day, people watch hundreds of millions of hours of YouTube videos and generate billions of views.

The video channel has local versions in more than 88 countries and available to navigate in 76 different languages (covering 95% of the Internet population).

Self-made YouTube stars share tips, reviews, how-to information and all kind of tutorials across almost all topics. The most famous stars include Jenna Marbles_with 17,620,623 subscribers, Zoella with 12,030,740 subscribers and Meredith Foster with 4,910,632 subscribers.

Other experts who have leveraged video on YouTube to build their brands include Evan Carmichael with 929,512 subscribers, Brendon Burchard with 598,227 subscribers and Marie Forleo with 416,835 subscribers.

The secret to their success? They just started and were not afraid to experiment. Then they consistently produced valuable content for their audience.

FACEBOOK

Facebook is currently the biggest social network worldwide[26]. As of the first quarter of 2017, Facebook had more than 1.94 billion global monthly active users[27].

Facebook is a powerful social network. Beyond enabling users to keep in touch with friends and family and share photos, the app is a big marketplace where businesses trade and generate substantial money.

Individuals and businesses use Facebook to build relationship with their fans

Facebook pages allow users to use the commercial features, making it easy to build two-way conversations, run contests and polls, offer prizes to incentivise readers to engage more and get people's attention.

Facebook Ads allow you to reach more people. It can be used to boost posts for more visibility, to find attendees for events, to launch a new product or book, sell products and services. You can find more information on Facebook for business.

Facebook Groups

Facebook groups can be used to offer extra support to your community. The group can be open or closed, and you can choose to keep it invisible or visible to searches.

Facebook Live

Facebook Live is the video streaming service of Facebook. It competes with YouTube and Periscope. According to mediakix.com[28], there were already 8 billion daily views for Facebook video in 2015. And now, Facebook Live videos are watched three times longer than regular videos.

Like other streaming platforms, Facebook Live is great to share live events with your audience. It increases viewership and engagement.

Thinkific Wednesdays is a great example of how businesses can use Facebook Live to educate customers or prospects. The online course hosting platform shares best practices, how to use the features of the platform, and useful tips to help customers create and sell their eLearning courses. Their series build a high viewership and engagement as they grow their community.

Jessica Gioglio provides further insight on how to best use Facebook Live and thinks that it's great for tip-based content.

"With Facebook Live, what works is around an event setting versus just arbitrarily going live. You need to make it like a destination and an event. So, announce that you're going to do an exclusive interview with someone at a specific date in time. I think you will get a lot higher viewership.

"I would say, maybe, once a week, do a Facebook Live for your company. Do an interview with somebody in the company about their job role or what they're working on. It could be a great strategy, maybe every Thursday at noon. Turn it into a content series, which is one of the biggest trends in social and digital marketing right now, whether you're a company or an individual."

INSTAGRAM

In April 2017, Instagram announced 700 million active monthly users[29]. Around 60% of Instagram users say they have discovered a new product or service on the image sharing platform[30].

The platform is becoming an important channel for businesses and brand seeking to engage their customers and audience with visuals like photos, video and stories.

Some businesses have been able to take off and spread thanks to Instagram. Those are known as Instapreneurs and there are many of them across various sectors.

Many brands work with social media influencers who have the desired following to drive traffic to their products and services. Etiquette is necessary when working with influencers.

Naomi Harris, a city worker in London, transformed her passion for fashion to becoming an influencer in her field. Her Instagram handle @thelondonfoxx has 19k followers and 600+posts. She covers lifestyle, fashion and beauty with a consistent brand of white and black glamorous atmosphere with flowers. She carefully creates her gallery of photos to match and attract the brands she loves.

How to Grow a Following on Instagram?

It pays to be thoughtful with your visuals. You need to have a style or a theme and create a consistent environment that will attract the followers you want. It should not be your product or service but an inspiring environment you create around them. When you have a consistent feed and people like one photo, they will like the rest because they are similar.

Make good use of the hashtags in your posts. There is a maximum of 30 for each post. Use them to be seen by relevant people and accounts. If similar accounts have bigger followers, engage with them by liking and commenting their posts. Their followers will follow you. So, be seen!

Contrary to some beliefs, Instagram is not just for kids and can really drive business. Mums like this platform because it's short. It's a visual medium, has photos and videos, and other people like them sharing real things, and it's easy to find people who love similar things who are willing to buy or recommend what they find useful.

This site moves quickly. You need to be flexible. Learn while you work in finding ways in building new skills appropriate for the digital age. Almost all sectors can benefit from being on Instagram, especially fashion, sports, art, decoration, food, beauty, health, etc.

In June 2017, the social platform organised its first event in Paris dedicated to Instapreneurs and to meet their fans while sharing their success stories and methods of growing their visibility. @Shantybiscuits, who designs personalised humoristic biscuits, has used Instagram to build her following across the world, whilst running contests and offering prizes.

SNAPCHAT

The photo and video sharing app reported 166 million daily active users in the 1st quarter of 2017.[31] The return on investment of this media is difficult to understand if your target group is not there or is more than 13 years old. But experts are seeing a brighter future with augmented-reality.[32]

"If your customer base is on Snapchat, you should consider being on there. Understanding how the platform works from a business perspective is hugely important because, Snapchat is such an innovator and I don't think we've seen the last of what they're going to come out with. As they continue to grow and evolve as a company, their age group could grow as well. I always tell people with any social media, don't put all your eggs in one basket.

"For example, Cisco is an old school tech company, but they've continued to innovate over the years. They do the coolest thing on Snapchat where they let employees take over their channel and do behind the scenes videos, showing what's happening in the company for a millennial audience[33]. But they're having people of all ages producing content for their Snapchat to excite millennial jobseekers."

—Jessica Gioglio

7. How to Measure Your Social Media Presence Effectiveness?

Do not be fooled by the likes and followers on social media. These are not real metrics, but weak connections. The magic happens when you create a real connection with people and not before. But such connections happen over time when you take the time to nurture the relationship.

Start building conversations and form relationships through consistent valuable content that engages your audience and builds emotional connections. It's about being intentional and strategic, which requires a well thought out plan to achieve your goal.

Stop posting random content and be deliberate from now on. Everything you do or don't do contributes to your personal brand. '**Make yourself findable.**'

Remember, when you join a social network, the best thing to do is to start listening, then add value by commenting and contributing before asking for help.

EXPERT TIP: Using Social Media | Jessica Gioglio

"You need to put aside a couple hours each week and focus on it. We all think we have to post reams and reams of new content, but it's about better-quality content over time. Fewer better blogs is actually not a bad strategy, especially when you're busy. Who has time for it all?

"Where I would be a bit more frequent is daily content on social media.

- **Facebook:** I don't do every day, only a couple of times a week. It's more quality versus quantity for me, as I have beautiful pictures to share of my travels and what I'm working on professionally. I do a mix of work and personal on Facebook.

"My Facebook audience are friends and family, as well as business people. I stopped separating the two, because I started going to conferences and people I meet at the conferences started friending me on Facebook. I decided to treat it as a personal and professional channel.

"I think there's beauty in that because when I was recently in Paris, I was in the Luxembourg Gardens. I love parks and gardens. I'm obsessed with flowers. They just lift my spirit. I posted all these beautiful pictures, then the next post was about business related things I was doing. I think that's the right mix. It shows you're a person, a human, and you have different levels to your life.

- **Twitter:** I do 3-5 tweets a day and I schedule them in a tool called <u>Buffer</u> that I recommend.
- **LinkedIn:** I do a couple of times a week about articles I'm quoted in, blog posts I've published or maybe something I find really inspiring. I really want it to be very high quality.
- **Instagram:** I do one post a day, but that's my creative side, because I'm a visual storyteller and I love photography. I just share photos of what's going on in my life, but I really curate beautiful photos to share and I also cross-promote a lot with what's on savvy Bostonian.
- I want to start a **YouTube** channel at some point. I would be opened to testing this platform, but this is where the struggle is. There are not enough hours in the day, but I really feel passionate about this.
- **Periscope:** It's a great tool for companies that are doing live events. If you know you're going to have a live event or a major announcement, get multiple Smartphones or cameras to record it for YouTube, Facebook Live and Periscope at the same time, and just have those devices all going at once.

"Everyone likes to absorb information in different format channels. I love to watch YouTube almost like I watch TV. I don't have a TV. I have a laptop and that's how I watch all my TV programmes. Now, I watch a lot of content on YouTube, like Netflix. Some people are only going to see your content on Facebook or on Twitter.

"Right now, Instagram is hot. But every channel has something different to offer. Look at where your customer base is and how you can adapt your message on each channel. It might be millennials on Snapchat, middle aged women on Facebook or a different demographic on Instagram. You have to know how that varies and adjust your content."

Check the 'Resources' page to read how entrepreneurs & experts connect with their audience.

Takeaways of Pillar #6 Connect with Empathy

- Find the best way to communicate with your audience
- Make your original voice heard
- Tell inspiring stories that connect with your audience, create a library of personal stories, create a memorable story and tips to make your story more impactful
- Create digital assets that attract your desired audience
- Choose your main social network channels

Pillar #7 Build Your Community

"If you want to go quickly, go alone. If you want to go far, go together." —African proverb

You've certainly heard about the Intelligence Quotient (IQ) and the Emotional Intelligence (EI). But do know the 'Connectional Intelligence' (CI)?

Erica Dhawan, author of "Get Big Things Done: The Power of Connectional Intelligence" talks about the power of connectivity, a new form of intelligence we develop by being on social media.

In a connected society, value gets created by the number of people you are connected to and the influence you have is linked to the community you build and who engages with you. This has been true before and is more emphasised now as the digital world is a networked world.

You can get a lot more done if you get other people involved rather than doing it yourself.

Earlier this year, I participated in an innovative collaborative work in a team of twenty-one people from ten nationalities. We helped a Silicon Valley start-up to create a roadmap for its international expansion. But rather than meeting in an office with people that know each other, we collaborated online to provide a detailed strategic insight and roadmap in only seven weeks. The team selection, the briefs, interviews and coordination were done 100% online.

A traditional consultancy approach would have cost the company more money, and would have taken at least three months to come up with less rich insights that we provided. The company was really satisfied with the results, which they used to identify new opportunities.

What is priceless in this experiment is the open approach: the team agility, the unique perspective and the passion of the individuals involved to solve a worthwhile problem.

Pillar #7 'Build Your Community' will show you how to build a community that cares about what you do and support you to achieve your goals faster. This means finding people who believe in your message, in your vision, and are willing to get on board and make it happen.

1. How to Build a Community?

"It's the followers, not the visionary who bring the vision to life. Visionaries need followers as much as followers need a vision." —Simon Sinek

The greatest currency in the digital age is having a significant community that cares about what you do. Whether you want to publish a book, write a column in a magazine or newspaper, speak at an event, launch a product or service, you are inevitably asked this question. 'What is the size of your community?'

Influencers, publishers, organisers and promoters will only consider partnering with you if you have a significant following and community. The paradox is you want the help of these influencers to build a community but they are only interested in you when you already have a significant community that appeals to them. So how do you solve this conundrum and where do you start?

A useful way to solve this issue is to use platform thinking.[34] In the book *Platform Revolution* [35], Geoffrey G. Parker, Marshall W. Van Alstyne and Sangeet Paul Choudary explain how digital platforms such as Airbnb,

Uber, Amazon, YouTube and Facebook have managed to take over the world.

One of the strategies these digital platforms use is relying on the Network Effect to achieve an exponential reach. The more users engage with the platform and like it, the more they will invite their friends to join them and the more it attracts other users to also join the platform.

The key is to focus on building your community by providing something they value. This means you should avoid talking to everyone, as we've seen in Pillar #2, and being super clear about the people you want to attract. Focus on a niche you are passionate about and other people are equally passionate about. Offer great incentives to attract them, to stick around and invite their friends to join the community.

CASE STUDY: Building the Most Influential in London Tech Community | Russ Shaw

A fun project that exploded beyond his wildest imagination

Russ Shaw came up with what he calls 'a crazy idea' after he left Skype back in 2011. It was the third lucrative exit of his career when Skype was acquired by Microsoft. He no longer wanted a full-time role, whether it was in a start-up or a big corporation. He was just about to turn fifty.

"I wanted to do something, because technology and the tech sector have been very good to me, so I wanted to give back something.

"I could see that the London tech scene was gaining some momentum. Our prime minister at the time was talking a lot about London tech and the adviser to the Prime

Minister re-branded Silicon Roundabout, Tech City. I was also hearing the mayor, Boris Johnson, speaking about tech, and I thought this was great to see the government and City Hall both promoting the tech scene.

"But where is the private sector? Where is the diverse group of leaders from the technology sector coming together to provide help support, mentoring, Investment, and promotion to what's happening here? That's where the idea came to me in the summer of 2012."

Russ then spent eight to nine months enlisting the support of his personal network.

"When I felt I had enough critical mass, I launched Tech London Advocates (TLA) in April 2013. It was one of those experiences where fifty people said they would come. I had some very good speakers lined up, and almost one-hundred people came to the event.

"I thought this would be a fun project, and literally from that point my feet did not touch the ground, because this thing just exploded beyond my wildest imagination."

A spirit of openness and inclusivity

"I wanted to make it very easy for people to be in the group. It's built on the spirit of openness and inclusivity. The only thing I asked is to come into the group, and have a fellow advocate make the introduction. Advocates introduce advocates. It's part of what's called the Network Effect, which I learned from Skype, a brand built on the network effect.

"I just make it very easy for people to come in and I asked them to use it as a resource to help us be consistent about messaging about tech, and use the website and social media.

To do that you introduce at least one new advocate and adopt the ethos that we are here to help each other.

"If somebody reaches out and says can you help me, we say yes. If we can't, we say I'm sorry I can't, but I will find somebody who can. It's a very simple premise.

"The ethos comes from my days working as CEO of a late stage start-up called Mobileway. It was a global business. My investors, who were Brits, were all based in Silicon Valley. So, I was going to Palo Alto once a month and I could see how open it was there and how they supported each other.

"The busiest VC [venture capitalist] in Silicon Valley, like Sequoia Capital, will always give you thirty minutes to hear your pitch. They usually say, 'no thanks.' But the 'no thanks' often comes with, 'Let me connect you to this person,' or 'I'm going to introduce you to that person because they might be interested in what you're doing.'

"It's that spirit of open doors and helping each other that I felt at the time in London was not quite there."

Start small and follow up

"I always say to people, throughout your career, meet people, connect with people, and follow up with people. There are wonderful tools today I didn't have twenty-five or thirty years ago. What would my day be without LinkedIn? What would my day be without Twitter? It makes it much easier to connect with people."

Follow up with people who've helped you

"Anyone who has given you help and advice along the way, always appreciate it. Let people know what's going on and how you can get involved, so it is something that can be learned. Some people are more natural at it than others. I learned this many years ago when I was in between jobs.

"I've been made redundant, restructured out of a role and suddenly you're out of work for six months and you're networking. I learned during those phases of my life that those networks are really important to maintain, to nourish and to enhance."

If somebody reaches out for help, help them

"If you can't help them you say you're really sorry, I can't, but let me see if I can get somebody to help you. That won't always be paid back, but more times than not people will remember it and when you need help, advice or whatever, those doors will stay open for you.

"That is human nature. Do unto others as you'd like them to do onto you. It's the Golden Rule. That to me underpins what a good networker is all about, the golden rule and that spirit of helping each other."

Networking, a no-brainer

"So many people I know would say networking is no brainer, we all should do it. But I've seen over the years that some people consistently do it and others ignore it. My advice to anybody will be you have to put time into it. You have to put some effort into it.

"Your return on that will be exponentially wonderful if you do it and do it properly. If you ignore it, if you're inconsistent or if you dropped it for a few years and suddenly say hey I'm back, you'll miss it because you disappeared for so long."

Russ Shaw is now among the movers and shakers in London's tech sector and appointed a London Tech Ambassador by the Mayor's Office.

TLA is now a collection of 5000+ digital entrepreneurs, experts, financiers, investors and politicians committed to selling the capital as a world-leading technical business hub. And it's also spread across fifty countries, giving birth to Global Tech Advocates, the new parent brand behind other local networks.

2. Define the Rules of the Game

We've seen how important it is to connect with people to build a great community. But we've also seen that the engagement of the community is what makes a difference.

A great engagement goes beyond replying to posts and comments. To become a great leader of your community, you need to engage them at many different levels.

The first step is to know who matters to you, who you want to attract, and who can help you reach your goal. We've seen that successful digital platforms use network effects to grow, but not all network effects are desirable.

There are good network effects and bad ones. You want to avoid the latter and encourage the former. For that it's necessary to **clarify the rules of the game** upfront and let people know which behaviours are acceptable and those that are not tolerated in your community.

You need to make explicit the rules of interaction within your platform and place rigorous governance rules and clearly state the consequences if someone violate your rules.

I love how Marie Forleo clarifies the rules of the game on her platform. Rule ten states'[36], 'We have a kind people only policy. PITAs, trolls and other ignoratos who demonstrate mean-spirited, dishonest or douchetastic behaviour are not welcome in our community or as customers. That also extends to any practice of ageism, racism, sexism or any other ism that's born from bigotry and hate.'

If we compare Facebook and Twitter governance policies, Facebook has a more controlled approach. It has a more stringent policy and likely to remove those who do not play by the rules. Users need to identify themselves to use the social network and the settings allow for more or less control of privacy.

Twitter, on the other hand, is often criticised for its open-door policy. This attracts trolls who use their anonymity to behave inappropriately, driving some users away and out of the platform.

You need to think about the right governance of the community you want to create, which encourages the desired behaviour and discourages the unwanted ones.

3. Four Levels of Presence to Engage with Your Community

As a leader of your community, it's your role to create the feel and culture you want to see. You also need to be fully present for your community. There are four levels of presence:

Be Present Physically

Be fully present for people when you show up. Show up in full and try to put aside other matters not related to what you are there to deliver. People can sense when you are half there and your mind is preoccupied with other stuff, whether it's on camera, on audio or face-to-face.

Be Present Emotionally

Speak with and from your heart, be transparent; don't pretend to be someone you aren't. People will relate to your struggles as we've seen in Pillar #6 with storytelling. When your community sees you are like them, they will connect even stronger with you. Show your emotions and also support them when things get harder for them.

Be Present Intellectually

Offer great value to your community before asking for anything in return. Help people in their journey and provide direction to move them further up.

Most people are in transition and it's important to realise this. People forget what they want, why they are doing what they are doing, what's next, and where they want to go. Help them navigate those periods and provide them your perspective.

When you eventually ask for help, be specific about what you are asking them to do. Do not be generic like most emails I receive who are 'writing to explore partnership' but do not say anything specific about what we have in common and why I should be interested.

Be Present Spiritually

Go beyond transaction and empower your tribe to believe in themselves and change their world. Help them find strength, comfort and motivation. Inspire the best in them. But be honest, you are not superman or superwoman.

You can be the one to save them from their chaotic life. Ask where they are going and get them to another level of clarity. Give them some aha moments and get them to think honestly about themselves. This will get you fans. Be a positive model in your communications.

People just want inspiration to cope sometimes, to see a role model to get encouragement that they can make it. People are looking for direction whether it's in your family, with friends or a wider network.

As the leader of the community, you need to support and challenge them to be their best.

4. Build Your Success Network

"You are the average of the five people you spend the most time with." —Jim Rohn

Throughout my career and during this research, what strikes me is how the most successful people have built and leveraged their community strategically to reach their goals faster and beyond their wildest imagination.

Who is in your network? Which level are they playing at? Do they inspire you?

A network is composed by mentors, advisers, coaches, peers, teams, and anyone who can help you to achieve your goals. Look upwards to people who are ahead of you. Look down to your team and younger minds. Look sideways for peers on a similar journey.

The Power of Mentorship

The best mentors have achieved success in what you are trying to do. They help you to fast-track your way and point you in the right direction.

Find successful people you want to emulate and either ask them advice or study them. Interview them, buy them lunch, and ask their advice.

Having a mentor that can teach you the ropes of the trade is key in accelerating your success. This is different than a coach who is not there to tell you what you should do. But they help you to give your best shot and hold you accountable to your success.

In the most successful start-ups, incubators, and accelerators, the mentors selected are part of the success of the start-up. They use their contacts to open new doors and enable their protégés to access a world they would otherwise not have been able to access by themselves.

But mentors can also be virtual. You can pick someone famous you want to model and study their biography, their philosophy and habits, what they did and how they did it. It's called modelling.

You can find a mentor anywhere: at events, on LinkedIn or in your workplace.

Antonia Anni, a user experience (UX) consultant, recruited her mentor online. To find a great mentor she says you have to be proactive. You need to do an honest assessment of yourself and see what you lack and find people who have them and ask them to walk you through them.

Antonia was looking for UX experts when she contacted someone who seemed like the perfect candidate online. After this, she established a relationship. When the time was right she asked the prospective expert if she can be her mentor. The answer she received was yes.

Antonia was relocated to London from Nigeria and her mentor showed her how to navigate the UK professional scene. Having someone from her background that looked like her was an important factor for Antonia. They have conversations on all subjects, including finance managing.

The Power of Coaching

Coaching is different than mentoring, but equally important to reach your goal faster. The coach doesn't need to be an expert. But it should be someone who has specific qualities to allow the coachee to push beyond their previous limit to get to the next level.

There is a reason why all great athletes and high performers have a coach. The coach believes in their potential to achieve their goal and provides methodology, structure and accountability to get ahead and achieve success.

Build Your Support Team

You need to have a support team, people who help you achieve more, people you can delegate tasks to rather than doing it all by yourself. Even if you are a solo-preneur!

I know it's not always possible to pay someone, but you can always barter and exchange skills with a range of professionals. Google 'barter skills' or 'skills exchange'.

A user on skillsbarter.com is expert in business coaching, training, management, strategic planning, counselling, and writing workshops. And looking for lessons in Photoshop, graphics and some other basic design programmes.

You can also use alternatives like internship, apprenticeship or freelancers if they are more appropriate to your specific case.

Surround yourself with the best people who share your vision to accelerate your success. Don't recruit friends just because you can't find anyone else. Do not hang around mediocre people – a mistake most people do when they start a business or a project.

You need to get out of your comfort zone. Put your ego aside and find smart people to help you. You don't always need money to recruit smart people. If you have a great business idea or offer equity shares rather than wages or fees, smart people will want to join you.

Get your community to co-create the future with you. People support what they create. Look for the most engaged people in your community, acknowledge them and promote them as ambassadors, moderators, etc.

Engagement is like a courtship. No one takes the other for granted. It's an ongoing seduction. Once you think you are entitled to something, it's over. You are out of the game.

Strategic Partnerships and Co-Creation

"A network of partners can rapidly scale your ambition."

Partnerships provide great value to scale up, but only when you have established some value. The first 6 pillars of YEANICC™ will help you establish a solid foundation you could then leverage.

Partnership is for leverage. It doesn't create value you don't have. No one will be really interested to partner with you, unless you show great value first.

Once you have proven value, you can then examine your key strengths and see who can be complementary to you.

One of the factors that limit the growth of a business or even a person is the mentality *'I want to do it myself.'* The truth, however, is you cannot achieve anything of significance just by yourself! The best and most successful companies are run at least by two co-founders or more. There is only so much you can do yourself.

To accelerate growth, you need to form partnerships and alliances to promote your offer. But finding the right partners is an art and a science in itself. It is the same as finding a life partner or spouse and it can take some time to identify the right person. This is why it's an on-going job.

Not all the partnerships work, but you can start with a clear set of criteria to limit the failures.

In a past job when I oversaw strategic partnerships, I developed a set of five criteria to build a successful partnership:

1. **Same Values**: The very first thing is you must have the same values. You need to make sure you choose a company or individual that matches your values to ensure you do not damage your brand. That's why you need to do a serious due diligence about that person or business, their clients and other partners to check that they are who they say they are!
2. **Define clearly what you want** and what you have to offer.
3. **Have an agreement**: define the roles clearly and establish who does what and when.
4. **Build Trust**: honour your side of the partnership.
5. **Maintain Relationship**: check in regularly and keep them updated.

I developed these steps to build a mutually beneficial partnership, and can be seen in much detail in my workshops.

Check the 'Resources' page to read how entrepreneurs & experts built their network.

Building an influential brand, as you can see from this section, is about showing leadership, building a tribe, offering help, getting support and involved in building your shared vision.

By being consistent and a role model, you will eventually reach that tipping point where you have a big community to support you and achieve an exponential growth.

The only secret to get there is **stick with it.** Serve one person like you'd serve a million and continue to deliver amazing value.

In the next chapter I will delve deeper in some of the key strategies to leverage your network, including how to build strategic partnerships to become a well-known expert in your field.

Takeaways of Pillar #7 Build Your Community

- Build a community and define the rules of the game
- Be where your audience is
- The four levels of presence to engage with your community
- Build a success l network and leverage the power of mentorship and coaching
- Build strategic partnerships with 5 criteria in mind

PART III: BUILD YOUR AUTHORITHY AND MONETISE IT

Building a personal brand in the digital age, should be a virtuous circle. You provide value and you get value. The more value you give, the more you get, or so should you. But there are people who give a lot without getting much in return and others who don't give much and expect a lot. Both approaches are losing strategies.

In order to get the maximum value out of your personal branding efforts online, you need to understand how to orchestrate your digital assets and the various strategies used to make money.

1. Building a Smart Product Suite

The first component of a well-oiled '**personal brand machine**' is to think through how to establish your authority. The online currency is quality content people love. It starts by providing a taste of what it's like to work with you.

Start with free content, also known as freebees or lead magnets, then move up to high priced product at the end of the scale. This is what I call a Smart Product Suite (SPS).

Smart Product Suite (SPS)
@FrancineBeleyi

1. Freebee & Lead Magnet

The first component of a smart product suite is the free content you create to share your knowledge and expertise with your prospective audience. This gives a first taste of what it will look like to work with you. It needs to be the highest quality possible that your audience loves and ask for more.

Think about some restaurants you've been to. If they offer you something to taste it better be something you love and want to come back to buy, otherwise there is no chance you will go back.

This is the same principle with your online content. Offer the best you have. Don't put out recycled information or anything that will not reflect what you are able to provide. This is not the place to get rid of what you can't sell or something that no one wants. Give the best you have, the most valuable content that will impress people to come back for more and eventually become a client.

The free content can be created in many different formats:

- Audio file or podcast
- Video
- Pdf
- Assessment tool
- Infographic
- Online course
- The best types of content are:
- Tips that teach how to do something fast
- 'How to' information
- Checklists
- Cheat sheets
- Playbooks
- Blueprints or frameworks
- Industry reports, market reports or consumers guides
- Quizzes

2. Entry-Level or Small Offer

Once your audience consumes your free content, they may look for more education. The next level of your suite of products is an entry level offer that is inexpensive. If they buy, it shows their real interest in your content and that they value what you provide.

This is the fastest way to test how serious your audience is about what you provide. Let them vote with their wallet. Entry level offer can be a printed book, an e-Book, an audiobook or an e-course.

The aim of the Smart Product Suite is to get your audience to invest more with you as they get great value from your solutions.

3. The Core Offer

The core offer is generally where you make the bulk of your money. It will be an offer you should promote continuously. It's your burger-fries-and-coke. Such offers include:

- **Offline programme** like a workshop, training, seminar, 2-3 days boot camp, or live events
- **Online programme** between 4-8 weeks which can include or not some coaching and hands on support

This core offer may include some of the elements cited in the point 4 below.

4. Others

You can provide other products and services at any of the higher price points in your smart product suite. These offers include consultancy or projects, done-for-you packages, passive income products, affiliates programmes, etc.

Consultancy or Project Work

With consultancy or project work, you help your clients directly in solving issues they face by providing personalised audits, strategies, action plans and sometimes help them to implement the recommended solution.

Let's say your client needs to grow their sales by 20%. You diagnose where they are now, what is working and what is not working and design the best strategy to increase their sales. Instead of stopping there, you can help them to implement that strategy, train their staff, etc.

Done For You (DFY)

The DFY is great if you can provide an all-in-one solution to your customers so they don't have to go through the learning curve and save time and costly mistakes. Here you don't teach them how to build it. You do it for the client. If your client needs a website, for example, you build a website for them (or outsource it to a specialist).

Passive Income Products

Passive income products are self-running programmes or products that generate money even when you aren't there to deliver them. These products can be e-Learning courses that run automatically. It can be audio programmes, home study courses, videos, printed books, e-Books or any other product that doesn't necessitate your intervention.

You can create those by recording the workshops, webinars, or any training you would normally run or create specific ones just to sell them as a product.

Any business can create e-products to teach clients how to solve specific problems and create an additional source of revenue.

Check MyDigitalPal.com to find a course on how to create e-products.

Affiliates Programmes

You can be affiliate for other programmes and get paid when people buy from your links or you can create your own affiliate programmes that other people sell. In that case, you give these partners a commission.

Many vendors run their own affiliates schemes but there are dedicated platforms like *clickbank.com* where people can promote other people's products or offer theirs to be promoted. Another popular platform is *Amazon Affiliates* where you can promote any product and earn money if people click on your personalised links to buy the items.

To make money on affiliate programmes you have to promote them extensively. Savvy marketers create niche sites to promote their affiliate links, as well as educating consumers on these topics.

Subscription Programme

Rather than selling one-off product or service to customers and hope they will come back, a subscription business model enables you to know in advance how much money you get each month, each week or each year. This recurring income allows you to have a more predictable income.

This is the model that mobile phone providers, Netflix, and many other providers use.

It's also easy for the consumer who knows exactly how much they will be billed each month.

The founder of Social Concierge, Nana Wereko-Brobby, has experimented with many business models before choosing a subscription model of £30 each month. The invite-only dating club for eligible Londoners provides the opportunity for members to get bespoke matching and attend private cocktail singles parties.

Today, many experts and gurus have their own subscription programmes that include coaching and mentoring as well as membership programmes. Members get access to comprehensive training, materials and support and pay monthly fees until they stop using the services. The more you provide hands on support, the more users get results and are engaged.

CASE STUDY: Make a Fortune Teaching Sewing | MimiG

MimiG[37] has created a highly profitable business that teaches sewing online. Users join her membership programme for $49/month to attend a new course each month. People can also access all the previous materials, from the very beginning level to the most advanced. She adds new courses as they become available on a weekly or monthly basis.

To provide further hands on support, she created a private Facebook page for members where she helps solve member challenges and celebrate their successes.

Her 3-day annual conference is a place for members to meet, show what they've created, and learn advanced techniques. The last day is a dedicated field trip to see vendors and new available materials.

The keys to MimiG's business success

1. She has created and perfectly executed the smart product suite model
2. She provided a unique course no one else offered
3. She delivers free but great content consistently to demonstrate her value and build fans
4. She engages fully with her followers no matter what
5. She leverages each social media channel like a pro. On Instagram, for example, she shares more personal visuals and behind the scenes moments than on Facebook

6. She plans carefully how she distributes her content and has developed a well-oiled system to measure success.

7. She is affiliate of various vendors and makes money each time someone buys from her links

MimiG's top advice is plan but don't' over plan. Stop over thinking and just do it.

"It's not about where you start but how you end."

It took her five years to get there but she is a testament of what is possible online with determination and perseverance. Your current circumstances have nothing to do with your ability of growth.

5. High-end Offer

The highest level in your smart product suite is reserved to your highest paying clients. This offer is an exclusive and premium offer. It provides a VIP experience for your top 20% clients and need to provide a high experiential value.

Typical high-end offers include a retreat in a 5-star resort, an exclusive networking programme with top people that your clients want to meet or an exclusive programme, highly valued by your top clients. It should be customised to suit the highest expectation.

ACTION: CREATE YOUR SMART PRODUCT SUITE

Use the steps provided in the playbook to create your own Smart Product Suite.

Having a suite of products is great, but how do you activate it strategically to make money out of it? This is what I will cover in the next section.

2. Monetisation Strategies

There are many Online Monetisation Strategies. These are the key ways people make money online whilst building their authority brand:

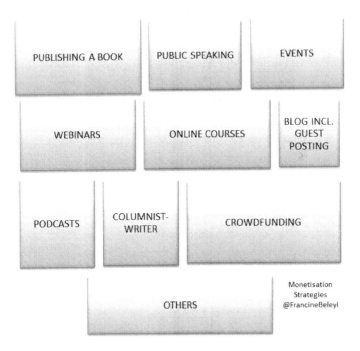

Monetisation Strategies
@FrancineBeleyi

PUBLISHING A BOOK

This section is not about how to write or publish a book, but show you the power of having a published book to accelerate your personal brand influence.

A book is one of the best ways to accelerate your recognition as an expert. A book can be published in various formats: paperback, hardcover, eBook (epub, mobi, pdf), audiobook, Mp3, mobile app, iBook, Braille, etc.

Publishing a book in the digital age is no longer the monopoly of a few mighty publishers who decide whether or not your book is worthy of being published or not. With the rise of digital platforms, it's very easy to publish a book. The main distribution platforms are Amazon, Barnes & Noble, Apple, Kobo, Ingram, etc.

There are three main ways of publishing a book today with pros and cons for each of them:

- The traditional publishing model where you need an agent to find you a mainstream publisher
- The self-publishing model where you take care of it all. The quality of self-published books can widely vary here.
- The hybrid model[38] where a professional helps you write, edit and publish a book to a high standard, providing more flexibility than a traditional publisher. Hybrid publishers include *The Book Midwife*, *Rethink press* and *Morgan James.*

Which route should you take to publish your book? Well, it depends on your objectives. Traditional publishing is still considered as mainstream and yield a greater authority, but you are locked in the way your publisher wants things to go. If you want greater freedom with full control of the pricing, marketing, and sales, self-publishing or a hybrid model might be the best options.

EXPERT TIP: Build Thought Leadership with a Book | Mindy Gibbins-Klein

Mindy Gibbins-Klein, Founder of The Book Midwife® is an international speaker, author, book coach & multi-award-winning Thought Leadership Strategist. She has turned 500+ experts into thought leaders and published authors.

How The Book Midwife® was born?

"Even when everyone has a book inside them, most people never manage to write their book, which means they need a bit of help to bring that book out. Having two children, the midwife metaphor came to me: If you have a book inside you, you need a book midwife to bring it out.

"It took me a long time to write my book and I've made a lot of mistakes. I didn't have any help and when I finally finished and got it published, I saw that there were a lot of people who were at risk of making the same mistakes. They really wanted help to make sure they wrote that book and did it faster and better than they would have done it on their own.

"The books that my clients produce are all brand building books. We don't work with novelists or with people who are writing for fun. It's a marketing related activity."

What holds people back from writing a book?

"A lot of fear usually holds people back, even people who think they are not fearful. There is usually some fear at the root of what is going on, which escalates to the fear of rejection. What if I write it and no one reads it or likes it? This then turns into the fear of failure. What if I write this book and don't finish? Then onto the fear of success. Oh my goodness! What if I sell a lot of copies and everybody is reading about me and I am exposed? And there are a lot of other fears as well. Am I good enough? Are my ideas good enough? Are people going to care, etc.?

"So, what I learned is we all have these fears in everything we do, but there is something about writing a full-length book that brings them to the surface. When people are trying to write a book without help, they are at risk of quitting or taking too long or really not sure about what they are doing.

"When they work with The Book Midwife®, they have more clarity and confidence. It's like partnering with somebody on something important. If you are training for a marathon or training at the gym, it's easier with a personal trainer. If you climb Mount Everest, you've got guides. There are some things that you shouldn't do on your own. Writing a book is one of those. It's risky."

What benefits your authors have been able to achieve?

"The reason our authors write their books is for credibility. You can build credibility in a lot of ways and there is something about a book that leapfrogs the others. It has a disproportionate benefit or advantage for the author, because everybody has a blog, everybody has a website, everybody seems to go on a stage and speak, but not everybody is writing their book. So, you still stand out because it's still a little rare. What you get from that ranges from being seen as an authority, you can raise your fees, and lots of doors may open.

"I had clients who have been on TV, who have been invited into major projects, who have been invited to speak at incredible locations. I had clients who had won deals because they had a great book, so there is a tangible return on their books."

Getting a huge sense of fulfilment with a published book

"My passion is to help people share their insights and stories. The book is one way and the other company I run is about helping people express themselves. The book is a very tangible product. It's a real way for somebody showing they are an expert and that they had something interesting to share. It's not the be all and end all, not the only thing, but it's really exciting, especially for people at risk of never writing their book. It's a joy and a huge sense of fulfilment for everybody involved when they actually do it."

STORY: Benefits of Becoming an Author | Jessica Gioglio

Jessica Gioglio and her co-author, Katrina Walter, got the idea of writing their book "The Power of Visual Storytelling" whilst on a trip to Paris where they were invited to speak at Le Web conference back in 2012. Jessica says it opens a lot of doors to become an author.

"There's just an amazing credibility about writing a book; and there are two sides of it.

"On one side, it's a little terrifying. We all have ideas we're passionate about and we want to bring them to work, but with that comes being judged. Is your book good? Do people agree with you? There are risks and rewards. We felt the reward was going to be higher because it was done in a professional corporate context. We're writing about what we've done at major companies and felt very confident in that.

"Writing a book gives you more credibility in everything, from interviewing for jobs to speaking engagements and giving me more ideas for future businesses. I did this while I was working full time at a major corporate brand. But a lot of people that are in consulting teach or want to do workshops and leveraging books as the credibility can do just the same.

"I have a friend who wrote a book on how to be a six-figure travel writer and self-published on Amazon. She basically told her story of how she started to make a six-figure income travel writing. She uses the book in her workshops and gives a free book away to everyone who buys a ticket to the workshop. And it boosts her credibility when she says I'm going to teach you and walk you through some of the key principles in my book.

"You do get a lot of opportunities that come to you, but you also have to create your own opportunities. It's not just like you write the book and the flood gates open. If you're a marketer, sales professional or business professional, it is the same tactics that you would use. You need a good website, a speaker's reel, certain elements to remind people that you're out there and why they should purchase the book."

PUBLIC SPEAKING

Public speaking is another great medium to build your authority faster. It's not always paid but can lead to new opportunities.

There are many great associations, such as Toastmasters, National Speakers associations, meet up groups to learn and master the art of public speaking. There are also plenty offline and online courses on Udemy, Skillshare or Coursera.

Speakers' bureaus for more experienced speakers include London Speaker Bureau, Speakers' Corner, BigSpeak and National Speakers Bureau.

How to Find Speaking Gigs?

There are paid and non-paid opportunities to speak. You need to consider what could represent a good opportunity to grow your business or just to give back, Jessica Gioglio says.

"I've written so much for a lot of industry blogs and my name comes up in Google for certain industry topics. I always ask people where they found me and they will say through a video they've seen online, but also through my network," she says.

"Get to know the other speakers. Tell them about your topic. You see a lot of the same speakers at the events. When people see you speak and think that you did a good job, they're more likely to recommend you when they can't do a speaking engagement.

"The trend now for speakers is to go through speakers' bureaus where they will work with an agency, which takes a commission fee to help them get paid engagements.

People really invest in a website, a speaker real video, which matches up a lot of your talks. There are niche websites now like *Speakerhub* and *LEAD.RS*, which you can apply to and register as a speaker. There are more and more websites like that whether you want to be paid or not.

"I would also recommend, especially when you have a website, to list the talks that you do, especially for SEO, so when people are looking for speakers on specific topics, they can find you.

"I have about seven talks that I regularly do and I always update them for every talk; I don't just use the same material every time I speak about influencers or content marketing, but I have very defined topics for my talks and it makes it very easy for a conference organiser to hire you."

EVENTS

To build a strong personal brand, you need to be a player. Be known by your peers, by influencers, prospective clients, etc. One of the best ways to get noticed by the movers and shakers in your industry and attract lucrative opportunities is to increase your prominence in your industry without trying too hard.

Events are great ways to meet face-to-face those who count in your industry and share your experiences. You need to be at the industry events where your audience go.

List which conferences your desired audience go to and be there. The more they see you in a familiar environment, the more they will like you. This is what psychologists call the 'mere exposure effect.'

Check out popular websites, like Eventbrite and Meetups, or the Internet in general to find the relevant events in your field. There are hundreds of events running in major cities every day, both free and paid ones. But be selective and know why you are going to a particular event and who will be there. Prepare in advance and do some background research to make the most out of them.

Hosting your own events is a totally different ball game and can yield a huge return on investment. When I was international marketing manager, running events was a big part of the marketing strategy of the company. We used to run events to generate highly qualified leads with senior executives and decision makers internationally.

One of the ways Russ Shaw, founder of Tech London Advocates, try to stay relevant is through the events that he organises.

"I do big TLA events twice, sometimes three times a year. I think about the themes of those events and decide usually a good six months in advance. I try to think about the events I host in light of what is going on now, so that we stay fresh and relevant. We bring the most dynamic leaders and speakers together for each of those events."

Events include product launch, workshops, seminars, lunch 'n learn, masterminds, annual conferences, quarterly meetings, morning briefings, gala dinners, awards ceremonies, etc.

Providing the platform for other experts positions you automatically as the go-to person. You get to build strong relationships with other speakers you've invited on your stage and they are likely to invite you back or recommend you to others. Such is the law of reciprocity.

Amanda Bradford, founder of *theleague.com*, a dating app for people with high standards, takes events' strategy to another level and creates long waiting lists before a new city is opened. For her 'a product launch is identical to throwing a party' with a lot of pre-games to build the excitement and anticipation.

She pre-gamed the San Francisco launch for five months with 8000 registrations and 76000 within 3 months of going live. She repeated the launch strategy successfully in New York and Los Angeles.

I attended her presentation in London, the next city on her list, to learn about her brilliant marketing strategy to recruit eligible alpha men and alpha women. Don't get me wrong, I didn't go to become a League member, but the request to register to the event made it mandatory to register on the app, so I complied! ☺

WEBINARS

Webinars are seminars hosted online. You can run them in the comfort of your own home using just your PC equipped with a webcam.

Popular webinar platforms are *YouTube live, Zoom, gotomeeting, gotowebinar, Adobe connect, WebinarJam*, etc. You can also use *Facebook live* as a webinar tool. All you need is a PowerPoint presentation or share your message live with no presentation support.

Getting attendees to your webinar is no different than what you will do for a seminar offline. You need to send out invitations, create an opt-in box to collect the details of attendees, get them to show up at the webinar, deliver the webinar and follow up with offers.

Sending reminders prior to the webinar itself ensures people don't forget. An increasing way of monetising webinars before the actual delivery is to offer a small item to purchase related to the webinar topic, but doesn't compete with your main offer.

If you offer a 4-week WordPress class during the webinar, for example, a complementary offer prior to the webinar is to sell a tutorial to record videos to share on your WordPress site.

During webinars that last generally between 45 minutes to 90 minutes, you need to teach great and valuable content to registrants and present your offer or pitch only after you have delivered great value.

ONLINE COURSES

E-Learning programmes and online courses are popular today. But what make a programme successful? Here are ten points to ensure you create and deliver an awesome course.

1. Provide **step-by-step framework,** processes and systems that solve a problem from A to Z

2. It needs to **flow in a logical fashion**: the fundamental aspects need to be covered first and the difficulty gradually increases

3. **Easy navigation**: the navigation in an online environment is very important and needs to be intuitive and easy to move forth and back without confusion

4. **Your style as a teacher**: how you deliver the lesson is important to connect with your learners; consider how you engage your learner, how you explain, your tone, your speed of speech, your pace, etc.

5. **Provide specific information** and not generic ideas: you can provide concepts to provide a big picture but

you need to give practical ways of doing a task and real-life examples that show how other people have applied what you teach

6. **Take them on a journey**: It easy to follow when we are taken on a journey and feel confident that it's leading somewhere rather than a collection of events without a clear connection between them

7. **Provide a roadmap** to follow: adults learn best when they know where they are going and what steps are involved so they can gauge where they are on that journey

8. **Assignments:** people learn best by doing rather than listen to theory, reading a book or watching a video. This is why an effective learning programme needs to include practical activities for learners to apply the learning to their individual situation. It's by applying the learning that it sticks

9. **Feedback:** People are likely to engage more with their learning when they get answers to their questions and receive feedback on how well they are doing.

10. **Community/team work**: A Stanford study shows that students on teams were 16 x more likely to pass their courses. When I run seminars or workshops offline, one of the best part is when people get together to solve each other's problem. Grouped or paired work is important to make the learning sticks. In an online environment, the same is true. Providing a forum where people can connect to share their experience, get feedback and solve problem is a must

It is easy to set up a course online today with plug and play platforms that offer the system to upload your courses and sell them. Popular platforms include *thinkific.com, newkajabi.com, Lynda.com, coursera.org, Udemy.com, codecademy.com, udacity.com, skillshare.com, novoed.com, fun-mooc.fr* .

CROWDFUNDING

'Crowdfunding is a way of raising money by asking a large number of people each for a small amount of money,' according to ukcfa.org.uk. It's a way to test your idea, pre-orders and funding.

I wrote a three-part series on 'how to use crowdfunding to launch your projects' featuring two journalists who explained how they have successfully crowdfunded their journalism projects.

Peter Jukes has pioneered journalism crowdfunding in the UK when he appealed to the crowd to fund his coverage of the widely publicised 2014's phone hacking trials and his first book, *"Beyond Contempt."* He then persuaded 1500 readers to 'pre-buy' his next book on phone hacking," 'The Fall of the House of Murdoch." *Martin Hickman* is an investigative journalist and founder of Canbury Press and co-author of *"Dial M for Murdoch,"* covering the #WallisTrial using crowdfunding.

Why Turn to Crowdfunding for Your Project?

There are many reasons listed below:

- **Quick and flexible:** a way to appeal directly to the public for funds
- **Understand your market better:** people ask questions and you have the opportunity to pinpoint their interests and refine your offer

- **Get buy-ins:** people buy what they support and if they help get your project off the ground, they are likely to buy your product when it's ready
- **It's based on trust:** to increase trust you need to showcase who you are, what you do, your past experience, and any relevant information you have that indicate you can deliver
- **Get additional help:** people love to help and will help you to check and double check your stuff
- **Establish relationship:** between you and the funders, there is no middleman between you and the audience, so it's easier to build a relationship
- **Solidarity with peers:** observations show that people often get support from their peers, such as artists backing artists, journalists funding other journalists, etc., perhaps because they know the reality and how difficult it is to get a project off the ground

Crowdfunding is Not a Get Rich Quick Scheme

If you know no one, you aren't likely to get far! Like all the platforms, a crowdfunding platform is a way to solve the inefficiencies, but not a magic pill where a totally unknown person will hope to get his project miraculously funded. It is not that easy and all the fundraising fundamentals apply here.

To make your crowdfunding campaign successful, you need to have a pre-existing, preferably big community that backs you up and commit to backing you up.

Don't expect journalists to write about your campaign and send press releases if your campaign has nothing unique or is not worthy of their attention. But if there is an element your local press may be interested in, it's worth shooting them an email.

Note that Peter Jukes had a massive following on Twitter before running a crowdfunding campaign to back his other projects. And so were many of the people who successfully funded their projects.

John Lee Dumas of Entrepreneur on Fire had his Freedom journal project funded on Kickstarter because he leveraged his huge community

Arianna Huffington's book "Thrive" was successful on Indiegogo because of her massive following and the marketing guru Joe Polish's large number of followers.

The Video Marketers Cookbook managed to get funded, but the author, Meg Le Vu, reported she had to go to great lengths and begged repeatedly her contacts one by one to just make it.

It takes preparation, planning and effort. And if it fails regardless, you will be able to collect a lot of insight and get some publicity for your activities. Crowdfunding can also be a valuable market research tool, saving you the effort to build something people don't want and move to the next idea.

Crowdfunding sites include:
www.kickstarter.com, www.indiegogo.com,
www.venturefounders.co.uk, www.crowdingin.com,
www.investingzone.com, www.buzzbnk.org,
www.crowdcube.com, www.fundingtree.co.uk,
www.Byline.com, www.fundingcircle.com,
www.crowdfunder.co.uk, www.seedrs.com,
www.banktothefuture.com,
www.kisskissbankbank.com/en, www.patreon.com

BLOG

I've talked about blogs previously in the digital assets. Beyond providing useful and valuable content, a popular blog can be monetised. It can offer further education just like Carol Tice, the owner of the blog Makealivingwriting.com does to recruit members for her other paying membership site Freelancewritersden.com.

You can also use your blog as a window to showcase your expertise and get paid to blog elsewhere. Running your own blog shows that you understand how blogging works.

To be able to monetise your site, you need to stick to a niche that has the potential of attracting an audience looking to learn further about your topic. It can also attract potential sponsors, but only when you have significant traffic.

GUEST POSTING

You can identify popular blogs in your field and offer to write or post content to create authoritative back links and get fresh new readers. Check sites that welcome posts by reading the menus or footer of the sites and expect your content to be edited.

Posting is often free unless you have been solicited as a professional writer or because of your expertise. But if you have a compelling content, you can add a call to action at the end of the post to make an offer to the readers.

You can allow other well-known experts to write on your blog to attract more audience. Ask also your most engaged readers and raving fans to guest post. In all cases, make sure you are clear about the terms and conditions.

COLUMNIST / WRITER

To boost your brand, you can also become a columnist or write regularly on your chosen topic for well-known magazines, newspapers or websites.

Such sites include Forbes, Huffington Post, Entrepreneurs, Inc. Magazine, TechCrunch, FT, etc.

3. Craft a Ubiquitous Marketing Strategy

To be seen everywhere without spending much of your time and effort, you need to use a smart integrated strategy to distribute your assets across multiple channels.

There are various types of marketing tactics including:

- Content marketing
- Email marketing
- Social media marketing
- Direct mailing
- Ads marketing
- Affiliates marketing

Each of these tactics can be the subject of a book by itself, but they go beyond the purpose of this book.

We offer tailor-made services to craft a personalised marketing strategy. Get in touch at Personal BrandingintheDigitalAge.com.

4. Online Etiquette

Having a strong personal brand online means some people will like you and others won't.

You might be abused or receive insults, and have to deal with negative comments or trolls, etc.

Another dark side of being online is to stay safe and know what to do when things go wrong.

How to Keep Safe Online: Cybercrime & Cybersecurity

Cybercrime, also called computer crime, involves a variety of threats you could face online. The cyber threats landscape is constantly changing but some of the risks an individual may be exposed are:

- Harassment, intimidation, blackmail, incivility, etc.
- Defamation, damage to reputation, exposure to malicious, offensive or unwanted content (viruses, spam, pornography, violence, incitement to racial hatred and xenophobia, propaganda, etc.), intrusive advertisements, hoaxes, fraud, blackmail, fraud or abuse of any kind.
- Object for monitoring, traceability, excessive profiling (impairment of privacy and digital intimacy, espionage).
- Theft of data: personal data, confidential information, intellectual property, etc...
- Theft of equipment (computer, USB stick, CD-ROM, hard drive, etc.)
- Destruction of values
- Identity theft
- Disinformation, manipulation of opinion, influence
- Misuse of IT capabilities
- Takeover of systems by third parties (hacking)

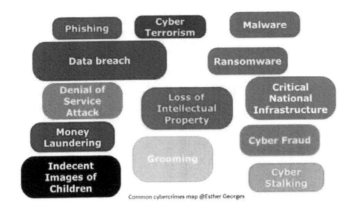

Common cybercrimes map @Esther Georges

Identity Theft

Identity theft is the use of a victim's personal identifiable information (PII), such as the person's name, birthday, and bank account number without the individual's knowledge. You need to take care of your PII and be mindful of what you post online. It starts by general security checks and measures as previously explained.

Another important consideration that we don't think about is to properly discard your documents using a paper shredder.

As a rule of thumb, do not open an email from non-identifiable source or file attachments you are not expecting. Lastly, you should not respond to unsolicited requests for personal information by phone, mail or online.

If you are in the UK, report it online to Action Fraud at *actionfraud.police.uk.*

Cybersecurity

Cyber security defines the mechanisms, policies and technologies to prevent cybercrime. A digital leader and anyone using digital tools should understand risks to their company, their assets and their investments faces in today's economy for an effective oversight and accountability.

Effective oversight also means understanding that cyber related risks are as significant as other critical strategic, operational, financial and compliance risks.

Without effective oversight and accountability, businesses are left vulnerable and cannot protect their assets from cyber risk and maximise their value.

Cybersecurity is a culture and needs to be inbuilt in our daily behaviour.

How to Mitigate the Risks and Dangers in the Cyberspace

No tool can protect us at 100%, but there are some useful tools and practices to help us keep safe.

The first step is to protect your computer with an antivirus, use strong passwords (not '123456' or 'password' ☺) and don't post personal information online.

The next action to take routinely is to backup all your data regularly. Use cloud solution to do this for you automatically, including your websites. Keep the backup secure. If your data is sensitive, you may choose to back them up on a separate hard drive and use a computer not connected to the internet.

The awareness campaign **Stop Think Connect**[39] offers materials in several languages.

How to Deal with Bullying & Trawling

Cyberbullying includes personal account hacks and posting, mean text messages or emails, rumours sent by email or posted on social networking sites, and embarrassing pictures, videos, websites, or fake profiles. Combatting bullying is not a one shop solution. It requires continuous action and education, but also strong regulation.

If you are a victim of bullying, report it to the platform firm, and if no action is taken escalate it to the specific body or associations that may be available in your country.

Key strategies to reduce the risk of being bullied are to exhibit self-confidence, respond with assertiveness, avoid the bully's tactics, don't isolate yourself and obtain support from others.

How to Protect Your Data: Data Privacy

As you collect information about your prospects and clients online, you should know about data protection, your rights and duty. I am not going into detail into this, but you can find out more information about what the law says in your country and in the countries where you do business.

- If you are in the UK, you need to refer to the Data Protection Act 1998.
  legislation.gov.uk/ukpga/1998/29/contents
- If you are in France, you refer to the CNIL *cnil.fr/en/rights-and-obligations.*
- In the US, refer to the Privacy Act of 1974 *justice.gov/opcl/privacy-act-1974.*
- The E.U is adopting a new regulation, GDPR.

From 25 May 2018, the General Data Protection Regulation known as GDPR will apply to you if you collect personal data from an E.U. resident (i.e. name, email, photo, IP address, bank details, medical information or any other personal information).

The individuals' rights include the right to be informed clearly about the collection of personal data and give consent to it, the right to access the collected information, rectify them, delete them and restrict the processing. The individuals also have the right to obtain and reuse their personal data for their own purposes, the right to object to any processing and the right to object to a damaging decision taken without human intervention.

You can find more information at *ico.org.uk/for-organisations/data-protection-reform/overview-of-the-gdpr/*.

If you operate outside of these geographies, check with your local regulator.

PART IV: MINDSET & HABITS THAT GET RESULTS

'Whether you believe you can or you can't, you will be right.' —Henry Ford

Many people know what to do to get better results in life, but often fail to do it. Why is that? There are many answers, but the two frequent reasons are because of their mindset and their habits. They want something but some of their beliefs and values conflict with that goal to get them the results they want.

This section provides the tools and tips to overcome the psychological blocks that may prevent you to take action and implement the YEANICC™ steps to develop the personal brand that will help you to achieve your goals faster.

1. Three Ways to Reclaim Your Power

Shift Your Paradigms: A New Level of Thinking

99.99% of what you think you cannot do can be done! Take Elon Musk with his crazy ideas and what he has been able to achieve with Tesla, SpaceX and the Hyperloop.

ACTION POINT: Remember something you once thought impossible but managed to achieve. What is it?

The mind creates all kind of stories that never happen! You are not your mind. Learn to control it, manage it and train it to relax and input new thoughts. Things are often easier than we think. The more aware we are of our basic paradigms, maps or assumptions, and the extent to which we have been influenced by our experience, the more we can take responsibility for those paradigms, examine them, test them against reality, listen to others and be open to their perceptions, and get a larger picture and more objective views.

Paradigm shifts move us from one way of seeing the world to another. Those shifts create powerful change. Many people experience a shift in thinking when they face a life-threatening crisis or deal with the loss of a loved one. They suddenly see their priorities in a different light. This also happens when they suddenly step into a new role, such as that of husband or wife, parent or grandparent, manager or leader.

"The significant problems we face cannot be solved at the same level of thinking we were at when we created them." —Albert Einstein.

We need a new, different level of thinking, often an **inside-out** approach rather than an outside-in approach based on what other people think we should do. Therefore, it's important to learn to know yourself, your strengths, your weaknesses. We often are convinced the problem is 'out there' and if others change, the problem would be solved. The truth is we need to take responsibility of our situation and **be the change we want to see.**

If you want a happy marriage, be the kind of person who generates positive energy, don't try to change the other person. If you want to have more freedom in your job, be a more responsible, a more helpful, a more contributing employee. Don't force your boss to give you a promotion. If you want to be trusted, be trustworthy and act with integrity.

The Power of Will

People can be mean online and you have to be prepared to deal with that. *Lizzie Velasquez* tells how she discovered a video online describing her as the 'ugliest woman in the world.' Lizzie was diagnosed with a rare disease that prevents her from gaining body fat. She was devastated to see such a video and with the help of her parents asked the owner to take the video down without results.

She decided to turn that negativity to fuel her dream. She is now a popular motivational speaker, sharing her story and inspiring others to realise their dreams.

No matter what people or the environment you live in throws at you, when you are self-aware you can be more detached and look at the situation like an observer. You have the power to decide how all this is going to affect you.

Between what happened to Lizzie (the stimulus) and her response to it was the freedom or power to choose the response she chose. Someone else would have chosen a completely different response. Remember, you have the power at any time to choose your response to what life throws at you.

Retrain Your Thinking

Even when we have all the tools to make a change, sometimes the wrong operating system in our mind prevents us to use them to make a lasting change. **A life of habits is not easy to change in a moment**. But you can retrain your mind. This is beyond the scope of this book. Neuroscientists, such as Jo Dispenza, have great information about unlearning and learning new habits.

2. Strategies to Live the Life You Want

Here are simple strategies to ensure you enjoy the process whilst building your personal brand.

Integrate Your Personal Life and Work

Your brand is you. It's not something you do from 9a.m. to 5p.m. and then carry on with your life. So you need to think through how you can make it work in life and at work, so you are not schizophrenic.

We have all heard the tale of successful business owners or high flyers who work so hard that they don't have any time to spend with their family or friends and have no down time to do any hobby.

With all the modern day demands, it can be hard to balance our life and work. The reality is that you will struggle to balance personal life and business when you are starting or growing a new venture, as your focus and determination to succeed drives you to work so hard that you discard everything else. But there is a way to integrate them both and make a conscious decision to do certain things that contribute to your overall well-being.

Arianna Huffington, the founder of Huffington Post, explains that we don't need to buy into the lie that we should be stressed out to be successful. I attended her 6-week online course based on her book, "Thrive." She shared her experience of being burnt out and warned against the belief that we need to be stressed out to be successful. We can set our priorities and give room to our well-being to keep us going for the long haul.

Building your brand is a lifelong matter. It's a marathon, not a sprint.

Who wants to do business with a stressed entrepreneur, a worn out executive or anyone who is not fully present and has various health issues due to a poor lifestyle?

Unfortunately, there is no free lunch under the sun – and we need to understand there is always a price to pay. We have to make that decision early on to have a healthy lifestyle as much as possible.

There are simple strategies that can work with a bit of discipline. You need to decide what are the most important things for you and schedule time in your busy diary to do those them, no matter what.

To give you an example of the domains to consider for an integrated life, here are some of my priorities and what I try to keep in check:

- **Early rising**: I am a natural early bird and can wake up at 4 a.m. if I've had enough sleep. I tend to sleep between 6-7 hours. These days, I mostly wake up at 5 a.m.
- **Connect to the source:** The first thing I do is write my dreams, pray and meditate within the first hour before I start my day. It helps me feel centred and have a sense of direction.
- **Physical exercise:** This is important for my mental sanity much more than to stay slim. If I don't do any

exercise, my body will let me know. So, I have built a routine with a minimum amount of exercise to do. I have a 20-minute exercise routine to feel energised and ready to start a productive day. I also exercise three times per week at the gym for 60-90 minutes.

I found a very good way to motivate myself to walk more. I load my phone with useful audio material and podcasts that I download from iTunes or my favourite websites to listen on the go. If you have the latest gadgets and can stream directly from your device, you don't need to do my extra step of downloading. You are good to go with your content ready on your device.

- **Healthy eating:** I cook from scratch most of the time and choose wholefood products as much as I can rather than indulging in quick take-aways. You don't need to be a chef - just choose simple good quality wholesome products, fresh fruits and vegetables instead of processed food or takeaways. I do not follow crazy or extreme diet, as I love my food and try to eat everything in moderation.

- **Connection/relationships:** I try to remember the birthdays of my close friends and family and schedule them in my diary, so I'd get a reminder on time and send them a message.

- **Time off to relax/ resource**: This one is the toughest one. I tend to work all the time, as it doesn't feel like work. But I try to keep my Saturdays off to go on a date with myself. You need to take some quiet time for yourself daily and at least one day off weekly to resource yourself.

Like many of you, I struggle to get these things right all the time, but it's always at the back of my mind and whenever I get the chance, I get back on track. So please do not beat yourself up if you don't follow this regime or a regime that works for you. But whenever possible, get yourself back on track.

Find out what is important to you and put in place simple strategies that work for you.

ACTION POINT: INTEGRATION WORK/LIFE

What are 3-5 things that are important to you?
- Connection to your source (meditation, prayer)
- Physical exercise (dance, swimming, walk, gym, yoga)
- Healthy eating (fruits, vegetables, wholefoods)
- Relationship/connection
- Security
- Time off to relax/ resource

List them and schedule a time in your diary when you can do them with minimum disruption in your life. Start small and increase the frequency and duration as you go.

3. How to Get Things Done Faster: Productivity Tips

Time is your most important asset. You can reach your goals faster when you are clear on your priorities. Focus on them and ditch the rest of your activities. Be strict with what you say yes to. You don't have to please anyone but yourself. Be stingy with your time and have a calendar to plan your activities ahead of time, and review them.

The **Eisenhower Matrix** can help to prioritise your actions. This is how it works. When you have a series of tasks to do first list them all on paper. For each of the tasks ask yourself the following question. Shall I do it myself, delegate or drop it? Decide if the task to do is important or urgent, then ask what will be the consequence if I don't do it?

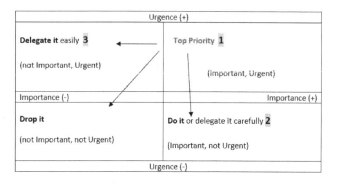

How to Use the Eisenhower Matrix to Prioritise Your Time

You can use the Eisenhower Matrix to prioritise all your activities, including planning your month, your week and your day. Please follow these guidelines.

- List your tasks to do in the tasks column
- There should be no more than ten tasks to list for monthly, weekly and daily activities
- Charge: Fill out this grid with less than 60% of your time
- Use Pareto's principle: Complete 80% of your goals and, if time permit it, do the remaining 20%
- Analyse the grid each day, week and month and see how you can improve your time management, but don't be a perfectionist.

ACTION POINT: USE THE EINSENHOWER MATRIX

Plan your daily, weekly and monthly plans in the playbook by using the Eisenhower Matrix principles.

SUSTAINING MOMENTUM

We live in an uncertain world where no absolute guarantee exists. If you demand certainty of outcome or success before you start, you will probably be paralysed. Even when someone promises you a guarantee, it might not turn out as planned.

If you accept uncertainty in life then you might accept that judgments and decisions can be made with no guarantee things will work out as planned. Successful people make their decisions based on incomplete knowledge and responsibly cope with the outcomes of their decisions and learn from each one of them to increase their knowledge for future decisions.

Instead of worrying about uncertainties in life, become probabilistic-minded instead. Think you will probably get more of what you want in life and less of what you don't want if you work smartly, take risks and are determined.

Building an attractive brand doesn't happen overnight. It's a long-time effort. It is a marathon, not a sprint and you have to be consistent in delivering your promises and building trust. Sometimes you might not feel like it, but you need to keep going.

How do you move forward when the first excitement has waned down and the going gets tough? How do you stay motivated to continue despite no sign of real progress?

Keeping the momentum is the cure for your inaction. Be persistent and follow through.

Look back at your 'big why' defined earlier in this book. Knowing why you are doing what you are doing and referring back to it will help you stay focussed.

Print your mission statement and pin it somewhere you can see every day when you wake up and when you go to bed. Keep it visible. Don't write it in a notebook or a file on a computer and forget it there. Use it every day as an anchor and reminder to stay the course.

One of the biggest challenges you may face on the journey to building your authority voice is to take action consistently, because you are doing this alone with no one to hold you accountable. Do not confuse freedom with lack of accountability.

Having no accountability can prevent even the most motivated people to progress faster in life. Studies have shown that people are likely to try harder to achieve their goals when they have expressed their commitment to someone else.

Like any champion or high performer who achieves greater results with the help of a coach, people I have helped to achieve their goals find that their commitment and accountability to me was one of the biggest stimulations to achieve goals that would have otherwise taken more time to achieve.

Get an accountability partner, someone who you tell what you are going to do in the month or week, and give them the permission to be a no-nonsense partner if you come up with excuses.

Accountability is a key benefit in our community, *Leading Voices Circle.* You can have one or many accountability partners to stay on track with your goals.

CONCLUSION

"No one enjoys great achievement without passing the 'Persistence Test." —Napoleon Hill

Power of Persistence

Those who have cultivated the habit of persistence enjoy insurance against failure. No matter how many times they are defeated they finally get there and often the view from the top is bigger than in their wildest imagination.

You will come across many testing times and opportunities to get discouraged in your desire to build an influential personal brand and quit. But if only you can keep going and pick yourself up every time, you will certainly get there.

Every successful person has once been a disaster. Henry Ford started from scratch and built an industrial empire of huge proportion with little else than persistence. Thomas Edison became the world's leading inventor and applied persistence to discover light bulbs and also one-hundred other useful inventions.

Other celebrities we know today, like Sir Richard Branson, Oprah Winfrey, Nelson Mandela, JK Rawlings, have all been through a lot of hardship but came up victorious at the other end. If they can make it, so can you.

In your journey of building a powerful and authentic personal brand, you may invest a great deal of time and effort with a return on investment not always visible. But make no mistake, there is a compound effect and all your little efforts will pay off beyond your imagination.

"It's not the big things that add up in the end. It's the hundreds, thousands or millions of little things that separate the ordinary from the extraordinary."
—Darren Hardy, The Compound Effect

Trying and failing is better than not trying at all. You learn from your experience and get better.

Before I finish, there is another invaluable lesson I learned in my journey that I would like to share with you. I advocate the power of goal setting and planning to achieve your dreams; however, I have to warn you about a trap that we can easily fall into.

Don't let the 'planning' stage of your goals overtake the actual 'doing' part. There is no need to perfect your plan before you take action. Follow the 80/20 rule. Once you have 80% of your plan done, act immediately. The other 20% you are trying to get right would not add much value, but you can waste a lot of time, procrastinate and never get things off the ground.

Have a plan, but do not cling on to it or make things inflexible. Remain open to possibilities that are coming your way and be sharp in evaluating what is a distraction and what is not!

Did You Enjoy This Book?

I trust that you have enjoyed reading this book, have completed the action points and will use the playbook to create your unique personal brand to achieve your mission.

What's that dream you are trying to realise? If you were to leave this planet today, **what is the one thing you would like people to remember you for?**

Don't be like some people who read a book and are inspired by it but do nothing. Inspiration without action is just hope. And hope is not a strategy.

Decide today to take the necessary action to live your dream, then take small steps towards it. Use the *Resources page* to download the sheets, the tools and strategies you need to plan your next stage in life.

And remember this. It's not about the destination. Enjoy the journey. Live and enjoy the present moment. Make it fun and worthwhile. Don't wait to be happy. Decide to be happy now! You have the power to create what you want.

This book is an ongoing journey of self-discovery and I am on a mission to empower entrepreneurs and other professionals to become a leading voice in their field, earn more and make a difference in their lives and in the world.

To thank you for reading this book, I would like to extend my invitation to join me in the *Leading Voices Circle* to share this journey together, access new materials, share inspiring stories as they become available, and get the support and encouragement of the community to support you to reach your goals.

It's my pleasure and honour to help you identify your passions and skills, do what you love with who you love and change your life and the lives of others.

I hope to have the pleasure of meeting you soon online or in person.

Until then Dream, Act and make an Impact.

Lots of love, Francine

P.S. If you enjoy this book or find it useful, I'll be very grateful if you post a short review and your success story on Amazon. Your support makes a difference. To leave a review, just go to your local Amazon page

P.P.S. Why not tell your friends about this book? Share this link *personalbrandinginthedigitalage.com* to get their copy and additional bonuses. They'll be grateful for it, I know!

P.P.P.S. If you'd like to share your stories because of what you read in this book or have any questions, please email *hello@nucleusofchange.com*. I will read it personally and will reply back.

Let's start on this journey together.

SUMMARY GUIDE

THE 7-PILLAR FRAMEWORK, YEANICC™, TO CREATE YOUR PERSONAL BRAND

Pillar #1 Know Yourself: Define and communicate who you are with empathy. It requires to be crystal clear about yourself, your passion and your motivation. Define clearly your life purpose, your values and what is important to you, write your personal mission statement and take further profiling tests to help you know yourself on a deeper level.

Pillar #2 Master Your Expertise: Find your passions, interests and skills. But following your passion is not enough and without real expertise no one cares about what you have to say. Find what makes you unique and if you are a MIMEC™, someone with 'multiple interest-multiple expertise and careers', who struggle to find one thing to stick to find an overarching theme.

Pillar #3 Know Your Audience: Determine with clarity who you care about. Create your ideal customer persona or avatar. Be selective to get a deeper understanding of their issues and pick the problems you are passionate about solving to make a bigger impact quickly.

Pillar #4 Lead Your Niche: Know the specific market you want to play in. Understand the ecosystem, the key players, the competition and what your role in that ecosystem is likely to be, so you can be the go-to person in your field. Create a killer USP and analyse your competition and the marketplace to find your ideal place within that value chain.

Pillar #5 Control Your Image: Take control of your image and your reputation. Just because you want to develop an authentic brand doesn't mean you should be sloppy, especially if you are positioning as a professional brand. Define your image, how you express your values and your personality visually. Determine your preferred style and colour that best expresses who you are and your unique tone of voice.

Pillar #6 Connect with Empathy. This is where you connect with your audience in the most compelling way. You need to pick your primary way of communication, how to make your original voice heard, tell inspiring stories that connect with your audience, create your digital assets, and build a smart product suite to build your authority and make money.

Pillar #7 Build Your Community. Build and leverage an engaged community to have an exponential reach. Find where your audience is and which social media sites you should focus on to achieve your goals faster. Build your success network and leverage strategic partnerships.

BUILD YOUR AUTHORITHY & MONETISE IT

Use the Smart Product Suite described in Part III for a sustainable way of building your authority with your content. Select from the various monetisation strategies the ones that you can quickly implement to make money whilst making a difference in your community too.

Adopt a strong online etiquette to keep safe, learn to deal with bullying and trolls and how to protect your privacy as you build your personal brand.

KEEP GOING

Part IV provides strategies and tips to sort out your mindset and overcome your psychological blocks. Create also an integrated routine that works to keep the momentum even when you don't feel like it.

The accompanying **Playbook** will help you to put everything together to design your own Personal Branding Roadmap in the next 12 weeks.

YOUR NEXT STEP

Visit the Resources page online
PersonalBrandingintheDigitalAge.com/Resources

1. Take the online **Personal Branding Self-assessment** to help you assess which areas you should focus the most
2. Download the **Personal Branding Playbook** to build your own roadmap
3. Access planners, worksheets and additional materials
4. Join the **Leading Voices Circle**
5. Get more help with one of the programmes below

Personal Journey
Start your journey to become a known expert today. This comprehensive programme will help you to create your expert status and attract more lucrative opportunities.
PersonalBrandingintheDigitalAge.com/CEO

Online and onsite training
Start today! Find out how everyone in your organisation can immediately add a higher value individually and as a team using the YEANICC™ framework described.
PersonalBrandingintheDigitalAge.com/training

Coaching
If you want intensive one on one coaching to help you develop one of the 7 pillars, get full support at
PersonalBrandingintheDigitalAge.com/coaching

Hiring
When hiring new employees, how do you recruit the right individuals and ensure the right fit for your organisation?
PersonalBrandingintheDigitalAge.com/HR

LEADING VOICES CIRCLE

The *Leading Voices Circle* is an exclusive invitation-only membership club with the mission to empower driven entrepreneurs and other professionals to be the leading voice in their field and thrive in the digital age.

- Members-only access to videos training, webinars, interviews with leading experts
- Monthly live calls where I share with you all my breakthroughs, new insights and lessons I've learned and answer questions you are struggling with
- Access to an accountability partner that will help you stay on track with your goals.
- Access to useful templates, worksheets and planners
- Network with people just like you over a weekend in London to take your dreams and goals to the next level whilst meeting people who can support you
- Bonus early bird: 2 tickets to attend a live weekend
- Quarterly boot camps on specialised topics
- Feature your profile and list your bio on the Leading Voices Circle platform directory
- The 90-day challenge: a quick-results programme of 90 days for people who are super ready and are 200% committed and can't wait to see results
- Participate in annual conference and meet other successful leaders
- Unlimited free support by email, getting interviewed, and featured on the website

Apply to join now at *Personalbrandinginthedigitalage.com*

INTERVIEWS

Experts and Entrepreneurs who have contributed to this book:

- Penelope Bellegarde, From corporate to entrepreneur | Founder & Digital Analytics Consultant at The Data Touch
- Milena Bottero, From struggling intern to entrepreneur | Founder Room for Tea
- Suki Fuller, Analytical Storyteller | Entrepreneur, Competitive and Strategic Intelligence Advisor, Global Keynote Speaker
- Esther George, Geek combating cybercrime | Cybersecurity and Cybercrime Prevention Specialist
- Mindy Gibbins-Klein, Book Coach | Founder of The Book Midwife®, International Speaker, Author
- Jessica Gioglio, Visual Storyteller | Author, Speaker & Marketing Executive
- Daniel Gurrola, Executive in transition | Telco Senior Executive
- James Saward-Anderson, Millennial hustler | Director of The Social Selling Company
- Riaz Kanani, Born entrepreneur | Business and Marketing Leader, Marketing Tech/Adtech
- Ekene Som Mekwunye, Award-winning filmmaker | CEO Riverside Productions
- Naomi Sesay, Media guru | Global Speaker, Head of Youth Media Engagement at Media Trust
- Russ Shaw, Building influential Tech community | Founder, Tech London Advocates
- Olivier Zara, From Military to consultant | Management & Social Media Consultant, Author, Expert in Collective Intelligence

Check the 'Resources' page to read their stories across the 7 pillars.

ABOUT THE AUTHOR

Francine Beleyi is a self-confessed MIMEC™, a term she has coined to designate people with Multiple Interests, Multiple Expertise and Careers. So, when it comes to create a congruent brand without confusing people,  what should you do? Francine's search to find out how to package all her passions, interests and skills (PIS) took her on a journey with insightful conversations with experts, entrepreneurs and leaders of the new economy. The result is a ground-breaking yet simple YEANICC™ model described in her book *Personal Branding in the Digital Age*.

Francine is a bilingual French-English, digital strategist, change & communication consultant, business advisor, trainer and speaker. She is the founder of *nucleus of change* and on a mission to empower entrepreneurs and other professionals to become leading voices in their field, thrive and make a difference in their world.

She has more than twenty years of international experience across Africa, Europe, USA, the Middle East and Asia, working for multinational corporations such as Total, Axa and Bnpparibas and supporting entrepreneurial initiatives, not for profit organisations and governments.

She holds a masters' degree in organisational consulting and change management, a bachelor degree in accountancy and finance and a degree in computer science. She also has an NCTJ diploma in multimedia journalism.

ACKNOWLEDGMENTS

I enjoyed writing *Personal Branding in the Digital Age*. It's been a long, exciting and sometimes painful journey to turn an idea into reality.

I am grateful to God, for the amazing blessings in my life and giving me the opportunity and wisdom to – Dream, Act and make an Impact.

Thanks to everyone who's helped me along the way and especially all the people I interviewed or discussed with for this book for sharing their stories and expertise. Big thanks to my beta-readers and anyone who provided early feedback and help in any form.

Finally, a big thank you to my editor, Shelley Young, for her professionalism and generous advice and others who have reviewed and proofread the manuscript and put up with my 'Frenglish'. Writing a book directly in English for a French native has certainly been a challenging but rewarding experience.

INDEX

END NOTES

[1] https://www.youtube.com/watch?v=VaRO5-V1uK0

[2] https://www.recode.net/2014/11/18/11632960/more-than-90-percent-of-u-s-households-have-three-or-more-devices

[3] http://fortune.com/2017/07/27/jeff-bezos-net-worth/?iid=sr-link3

[4] http://www.telegraph.co.uk/finance/yourbusiness/11782294/Mumpreneurs-generate-7bn-for-the-UK-economy.html

[5] http://www.oprah.com/inspiration/tony-robbins-why-we-do-what-we-do-the-6-human-needs

[6] http://www.dailymail.co.uk/femail/article-4262328/ANGELA-LEVIN-mother-cruel-horrid-woman.html

[7] https://community.arm.com/servlet/JiveServlet/previewBody/10926-102-1-22184/ARM_1st_Press_Release.pdf

[8] http://www.myersbriggs.org/

[9] https://www.eclecticenergies.com/enneagram/test-2.php

[10] https://www.enneagraminstitute.com/how-the-enneagram-system-works/

[11] http://wdprofiletest.com/home/?a_aid=nucleuswealth

[12] http://www.kolbe.com/

[13] Kathy Kolbe https://www.youtube.com/watch?v=eeajTMiA4pU

[14] https://www.theguardian.com/careers/2016/oct/13/will-jobs-exist-in-2050

[15] http://www.cnbc.com/2016/06/06/diamond-foundry-2016-disruptor-50.html

[16] http://www.selfridges.com/GB/en/content/our-heritage

[17] http://www.cnbc.com/2016/06/07/wework-2016-disruptor-50.html

[18] http://rogerjameshamilton.com/

[19] https://www.virgin.com/company

[20] https://www.fonts.com/content/learning/fontology/level-1/type-anatomy/serif-vs-sans-for-text-in-print

[21] https://www.statista.com/statistics/274050/quarterly-numbers-of-linkedin-members/

[22] http://reidhoffman.org/linkedin-pitch-to-greylock/

[23] https://www.statista.com/statistics/282087/number-of-monthly-active-twitter-users/

[24] https://www.omnicoreagency.com/periscope-statistics/
[25] https://www.youtube.com/yt/press/en-GB/statistics.html
[26] https://www.statista.com/statistics/272014/global-social-networks-ranked-by-number-of-users/
[27] https://www.statista.com/statistics/264810/number-of-monthly-active-facebook-users-worldwide/
[28] http://mediakix.com/2016/08/facebook-video-statistics-everyone-needs-know/#gs.lyg=tSY
[29] https://www.statista.com/statistics/253577/number-of-monthly-active-instagram-users/
[30] https://business.instagram.com/blog/500000-advertisers/
[31] https://www.statista.com/statistics/545967/snapchat-app-dau/
[32] http://adage.com/article/digital/snapchat-s-dancing-hot-dog-means-future-ar/309875/
[33] https://blogs.cisco.com/lifeatcisco/oh-snap-cisco-employees-takeover-snapchat
[34] http://www.francinebeleyi.com/voyage-in-the-land-of-platform-businesses/
[35] https://www.amazon.co.uk/Platform-Revolution-Networked-Transforming-Economy/dp/0393249131
[36] https://www.marieforleo.com/how-we-roll/
[37] https://www.thinkific.com/resources/mimi-g-teaching-sewing-online/
[38] https://www.publishersweekly.com/pw/by-topic/authors/pw-select/article/66658-not-all-hybrid-publishers-are-created-equal.html
[39] https://www.stopthinkconnect.org/tips-advice/